December 2018

Dear Sarah:

My son Travis had asked me to share this with you ~ my mum, like yours lived through WWII in England ~

This is the story of the struggles of the women that lived through such tough times.

I know you are now caring for your mum, as I did mine. It was such an honor to be able to be with the ending years of her life.... they really were "our greatest generation."

Best Wishes

Daphne

THE LAST *Gift*

DAPHNE MADDISON

WESTBOW PRESS®
A DIVISION OF THOMAS NELSON & ZONDERVAN

WestBow Press books may be ordered through booksellers or by contacting:

WestBow Press
A Division of Thomas Nelson & Zondervan
1663 Liberty Drive
Bloomington, IN 47403
www.westbowpress.com
1 (866) 928-1240

ISBN: 978-1-9736-2450-9 (sc)
ISBN: 978-1-9736-2449-3 (hc)
ISBN: 978-1-9736-2451-6 (e)

Library of Congress Control Number: 2018903881

Print information available on the last page.

WestBow Press rev. date: 04/17/2018

INTRODUCTION

On September 11, 2015, Patriot Day in America, Arthur Gordon Royle left this earth and went to heaven. His last gift was to be found 46 days later.

Who would have ever thought that at 93 years of age, with a rambling sentence about **never holding that baby** would turn out to be the gift of a sister, his last gift to his family; the sister they never knew they had.

CONTENTS

CHAPTER 1

A Special Birthday, March 5, 2013

Ten Simple Words Uncovered a Secret Kept for 68 Years

The room was warm and cozy; a blazing fire had been lit all day to keep out the chill from the weather outside; it was a room full of pictures, of family memories past and present, of happy times. Their home had always been a place to gather for all family occasions; they were the glue that held their family together, the cement that seemed to bond them all in good times and in bad. It was late in the afternoon, when everyone gathered to celebrate their youngest daughter's birthday; a birthday none of them would ever forget.

Outside the sky was dark and overcast; a light rain had been falling most of the day, the type of rain that just wets you enough that you can't get warm. The dull, grey clouds above would surely mean more bad weather to come; something that was so seldom seen in the sunshine of California in March.

Some 60 years before, Arthur and Margaret had arrived as a young couple from England in the mid-1950s, to raise their family in the "Land of Opportunity," America. Through hard work and loving hands, they had succeeded beyond all their expectations; their entire life they had created a close-knit family who seemed always to be there for one another. They had three children, two girls and a boy, and a multitude of grandchildren; and when they were all together it could be quite chaotic, but Arthur and Margaret loved their times with them, it was times like this they lived for.

As they sat by the fire, surveying the family that was theirs, age had rapidly crept up on them, the twilight of their years to be shared surrounded by those they loved so dearly. They had been together now almost 68 years, through good times and bad, and this was one of the good ones; their youngest, Elaine, was celebrating her birthday. She had been the baby no one expected, the change-of-life baby, their final child, and she was cherished far beyond words by the both of them. Where and how did all the years go? They had asked themselves that over and over that day; 52 years since their last child was born!

As the family gathered round, next to the warmth of the crackling fire, the conversation had started out innocently enough, everyone trying desperately to help their father with his memory, which was so rapidly slipping away to Alzheimer's. This once wonderfully funny man, who had told the best of stories, and who had taken such good care of his family, their patriarch, was losing his mind so quickly and there was little they could do to help, other than to be there for him; to touch him, and hold him, and share with him the memories of past happy times. Piece by piece of the person he once was disappearing with each day; as he was slipping away into a world of his own; the tragedy of losing him this way seemed far worse than anything imaginable that could be inflicted on someone who had been so good to others. He was a man who had been a wonderful son to his mother, a loving and devoted husband to his wife, and a good and protective brother to his sisters, Lily, Irene and Kathleen; but to his three children, a Dad was what he had been best at. He was a man who led by the example of love, and of hard work, he was a Dad who always made you feel safe, like nothing bad could ever happen because he was there. He was the Dad who spent endless hours running up and down a field, helping them learn to fly the kite he made for them; a Dad who would sit up all night and hold them when they were sick; a Dad who encouraged them with any sport they chose, and who stood on the sidelines cheering them on; he was a Dad who rose before the sun to get them to swim practice before he left for work; he was the type of Dad the movies write about.

He had never been a tall man, standing only 5'7" in his prime, but he had always been able bodied; helping every family member with any task that was called for. Even in his nineties, struggling with a walker to get around, he had wanted to help. He was a handsome man his entire life, even now, he had not lost the twinkle in his beautiful pool blue eyes. However, the Alzheimer's was taking its toll, and he was rapidly becoming more frail and weak, his hands had once been so strong, these had been the hands of a man that had been gentle enough to pick up a child to love them when they cried; the hands of a man who would build a home for his family; a man who never faltered in his love and commitment in caring for others; and now, they were the hands of a man, who at 93, needed holding.

Arthur could very often remember far back in his memory, way back to his childhood days in England; back to the war years, his time spent in India and Africa during World War II, and yet this particular day he was really struggling. With all the hustle and bustle that was going on in the room that afternoon, he was confused even more than normal; so to help him understand the birthday they were celebrating that day, they asked him, "Tell us a story about Elaine when she was a baby;" with a quizzical look in his eyes, almost as if he was trying to identify what was being said, he gazed around the living room at all their faces, then towards the windows, and the rain drizzling down outside; Something seemed to trigger his memory, as things often did....had it been the rain hitting the windows, ***was it raining the day she told him?*** He seemed to hesitate as he looked back; then slowly came his response, a response that was about to rock their family's world; ten magic words were uttered from his lips: **"I never saw that baby, I never held that baby."** His mind had been so muddled in a myriad of thoughts and then, out of nowhere, a sentence that made absolutely little, if no sense, to anyone in the room **except one person, his wife Margaret.** It was not unusual that he could not remember things, but then a sudden sob turned all their heads in one direction; with tears streaming down her cheeks, she buried her face in her hands, her sobbing voice cracking with emotion, as she whimpered, **"You promised you would never tell!"**

CHAPTER 2
Hearts Broken, May 8, 1945

A Forbidden Love!

Victory in Europe was declared, 1945 was the year World War II had ended; the Battle of Britain was over, finally the bombs had stopped falling from the dark skies above, Germany had finally surrendered. England had been left in total devastation with all of its major cities being attacked, houses and businesses were destroyed; they had been brought down to rubble and dust, so many thousands of lives were in ruin. Six years of anguish and suffering, all for a people to defend their nation, to stop the tyranny of Hitler. The hundreds of thousands of men who had been deployed in 1939 would soon be returning home from the front lines; but so many thousands would not, leaving family upon family to try and rebuild what little was left of their lives. A quiet had come over England for the first time in many years; no more "doodle" bombs from the enemy planes above, no more air raid sirens shrieking in the middle of the night, no more homes and factories on fire, no more people screaming in pain and agony; broken buildings and broken people, brick by brick, one day at a time, that's what it would take for years to come. The blackout drapes and tape that had covered all the windows in every business and home was slowly being removed, and the light of day would once again shine into their houses and England would arise from the ashes of war.

It is hard for our generation, or any generation, to realize what this nation of people lived through. They were called "the Greatest

Generation," and no truer words could describe those men and women who survived WWII, the agony of never knowing if you would see another day. Houses and towns were bombed and left burning around you, the rubble of ruined buildings was everywhere, the tracks of the trams were bent and twisted from the power of bombs that had exploded from the enemy planes above; walking or bicycles were the only mode of transportation for most, bar the army vehicles with special tires to climb over the mountains of bricks and debris, even buses had come to a standstill in all the major cities that had been targeted. The separation of children from their parents, as so many had been sent from harm's way in the big cities to the countryside or even out of the country itself; the loss of fathers, husbands, brothers and sons from their families as they went off to war, only to return to no home and sometimes no family; all could be lost with the drop of just one bomb. The shortage of food, as everything was rationed, and would remain so for years after. The war that Germany waged on the world was one that we today could never imagine.

Year after year, since 1939, more and more devastation would fall on this little country, a country small enough it could fit inside California; but so mighty, it would conquer the monstrosities of Hitler.

The women left on the home front worked in factories, building parts for planes, to help with the war effort. It would be the women who would assemble the bombs in the munition factories, or put the rivets in the spitfire planes so they could fly and fight off the German Luftwaffe air force. They were told to "**keep the home fires burning**," to stay strong for when their men would return; this was not just a war for men to fight, but a war that entire families had to pull together to create a united front ~ a Great Britain ~ to fight the oppression that had swept all through Europe. England was the last part of that continent for Hitler to conquer, and then it all would belong to him and his Aryan Reich; America would be next.

There was little food to be had during those war years; hunger was just something you grew accustomed to. If you were fortunate, maybe one egg a week for a family, mostly bread and potatoes were to sustain the greater part of England and Europe. Horsemeat or rabbits were a rare luxury, if the butcher had any hanging in his shop, and if you had enough coupons in your ration book, maybe, just maybe, you might get a little to make a stew. Babies were born at home by the front room fire, the hospitals were full of sick and wounded from the bombings; if you were lucky, a midwife would ride her bike out to your home, and hopefully, was just in time to help with the birth, very often by candlelight. If the street had been bombed there would be no electricity, and that was the norm, the daily life of what the people of England had grown accustomed to.

Two years earlier in 1943, at the age of 18, a young, beautiful woman sat at her dressing table, staring into the mirror in her bedroom, brushing her long, brown hair, contemplating what next to do with her life. She lived in a terrace house, a typical two rooms upstairs, two rooms down, that had been built at the turn of the century, 1900, when Queen Victoria's husband, Albert, had decided everyone should have their own home, even if they were attached. Margaret's bedroom was upstairs in the back of the house, overlooking the tiny victory garden, full of vegetables that they had recently planted; her room was so little and dark; since the outbreak of the war, even the windows had been darkened with blackout curtains. With ugly, dull, flowered wallpaper, that had been on the walls ever since she could remember; still this was her sanctuary, the only place in the house she could go to escape, and forget the day to day drudgery of living with her mother. Margaret had to stop daydreaming; for soon, her mother would be home from the pub, and she knew she had to get downstairs and start the tea or it would be a clap across the face for her, as usual. She had finished her morning shift at the factory and was home most days early enough to start the evening meal and clean the house. Her mother didn't work, but seemed to always have enough money to make it to the pub for several pints of beer, and yet continually had her hand out to Margaret to take the small pay packet she received from the biscuit factory where she worked.

Everything around her had changed dramatically since the outbreak of the war; most of her friends had gone in so many directions; all the men had either volunteered or had been drafted to fight for their country, at least all the boys she had been dating. Margaret had decided she was tired of the quarreling in the house; the angry words from her "Mam" only had seemed to intensify as the months went on. She and her mother had lived alone in Manchester; her father had recently died, and this had left Margaret at a loss what to do with her life, days seemed just without purpose; her mother was always out drinking or at home sleeping it off. If she was awake, she was always so angry and Margaret was the one who got the blunt end of that rage. As she gazed into the dull mirror on her dresser, she had come to a decision while daydreaming, "Yes, that was it," she proclaimed out loud, "I will enlist!" Margaret decided to do her part and wear the uniform of the W.A.F. (Women's Air Force). With grandiose ideas that befall young people, it all seemed so glamorous, the uniform, the men, freedom at last from the shackles of her home!

She took extra pride early the next morning while dressing, she only owned four dresses, so she picked the one she felt flattered her the most, the one with the flowers, it was bright and cheery and the color suited her mood. As she left her house at the crack of dawn, her mother still asleep in bed from a late night at the pub, she quickly grabbed her dark green coat from the hall rack, and quietly snuck out the front door, so her Mam would not hear her leave; trying desperately to close the creaking, old door silently behind her, as she had done so many times before, to avoid the rantings and ravings of her mother.

Running up the street to catch an early bus, she felt a sense of joy and independence, something she had not felt in a long time. As the bus pulled up and Margaret jumped on board, paid for her ticket with the few coins she had left in her pocketbook, she then headed up the stairs, her favorite place to sit, so she could have a smoke, like all the other young people of her generation. Staring out the window from the front of the bus, as she lit her cigarette, she couldn't help but wonder, what would her mother think? What would she do? Smiling at her, across the aisle, she caught the eye of a soldier, who must have been on leave; she knew she was pretty, and the attention she got made her feel even more so. "Yes", she thought to herself, "this was going to be a brilliant day." She had managed to sneak out undetected by her Mam, and now the big, red double-decker bus was headed down Stockport Road in the direction of the recruiting office at the local town hall, and there was nothing her Mam could do; after all, she was 18, and needed no one's permission. Margaret was anxious to get away from her mother's drunken tirades at home and this was the perfect opportunity.

Her enlistment papers had been signed that morning at the Town Hall, which had been turned into a recruiting office since the outbreak of war; before Margaret arrived home, her mother had woke from her drunken slumber, looking around the house for her daughter, annoyed that the fire in the front parlor was not lit to warm the room; when all of a sudden the front door opened and there she was, Margaret all dressed and smiling. The angry accusations started all over again, "Where have you been? What have you been up to?" bellowed her mother. As Margaret ran up the stairs, past her mother, not even taking her coat off her back, she slammed her bedroom door shut, only to have it thrust open by the woman she wished was not her Mam. "I'm leaving!" Margaret exclaimed. As her mother raised her walking cane and slammed it across her daughter's head, she went flying to the floor, with tears in her eyes and a dizzy feeling in her brain; Margaret decided that she could not wait to leave this nightmare called home. Her mother stormed out of her bedroom before Margaret managed to pull herself up off the floor and onto her bed; rubbing the side of her head, she now knew she had made the right decision and leaving couldn't come soon enough.

Weeks had passed before her paperwork had come in the mail from the Air Force; the date had finally arrived, and not too soon, as the mood at home had only gotten worse since her mother had found out she was leaving. It was late morning when Margaret finished packing her bags to leave, by then the house was empty. A quick walk up the street to catch the number 7 bus to downtown Manchester Train Station, and she would be free of the shackles of her mother's home. When she arrived at the station, with a small suitcase in hand, the London Road Depot was bustling with people. She boarded the train alone that day, her mother had chosen a trip to the pub that morning instead; Margaret knew her Mam was angry and a trip to the pub was nothing new; a pint had always meant more to Rebecca Podmore than her family had. She had left without even saying goodbye to her only daughter, with anger and malice in her heart, she had no desire to show any affection one way or another to Margaret.

She knew it would take a good part of the day to get down to the base where she was to be stationed; there would be many stops along the way. The trip would mean a change of trains, then on over to Lincolnshire, followed by a bus ride to the barracks. She looked out the window at the beautiful countryside, miles of green rolling hills and pastures, and at the trees, just as they were starting to blossom, with spring on the way. She felt calmness come over her, as the train took her farther and farther away from the life and the woman she detested. Margaret had managed to sneak some bread out of the pantry and packed a sandwich to hold her over, until she arrived at what would be her home for the next year. She was posted at a base called RAF Strubby, near the little town of Alford; this particular Royal Air Force Base was located on the east coast of the midlands, the area is flatland, and a perfect place for the bomber planes to cross the channel and drop their explosives on Germany. Many of the major squadrons would fly out of this airfield, which was originally opened during the war because of its strategic location.

Arriving at the base, she got off the bus with the rest of the new recruits, just a handful of young women, excited at their first venture of freedom into an adult world; really not realizing what they were about the embark on. With suitcases in hand, they were all directed into a small green hut, and would from there be checked into the base and assigned different jobs. Each was given a smart uniform with brass buttons up the front, along with a shirt, tie, and cap for their heads. As she was assigned to her barracks, Margaret quickly made friends with three other girls, all about the same age, and a new adventure to her life was about to begin.

In June 1941, approval had been given to construct an airfield at Strubby. It was closer to occupied Europe than any other airfield; and so three surfaced runways, and three hangars were put into place. Strubby was a place surrounded by mile after mile of countryside that encompassed acres of flatlands, but because it was close to the North Sea, it was austere, cold and damp; not a place you would want to be in winter; somewhat like the weather in Manchester, but much colder, as the arctic winds blow down from the North Sea. It was hard to imagine what would go on here; the importance of this base was vital in playing a special strategy in ending the war. Big towns were what the Germans were in search of. The bombs would drop on London, Manchester and Birmingham, or on the docks of Liverpool and Newcastle, but not the little villages like Alford in Lincolnshire.

Margaret Podmore
Women's Air Force, 1943

When early morning came in the barracks where the girls were assigned to sleep, Margaret woke up with a smile; she had a new purpose in life and a peace in her heart. She had left her mother behind, her ugly drinking and unkind words, it was all like a bad dream that she no longer had to endure. Her newly assigned uniform was so smart, a kind of blue-grey color with nationality shoulder flashes representing the W.A.F. on the upper arm. As she and the other girls made their way to the canteen in the dark of the morning, she could hear the humming of planes in the distance, wondering if it was the enemy ready to drops their bombs; or one of their own, landing back at base.

As she entered the canteen, all eyes turned, and she smiled at the troops eating breakfast, each man readying himself to fly out that morning; she knew then that she had made the right decision enlisting. The days were busy and long; her job was an important one, or so she felt. Margaret, along with one of the other new girls, had been assigned to work in the War Rooms. There really was not much time for training new recruits; the war had been going on now for five years, since 1939, and you were thrown right into the mix and expected to learn quickly whatever your duty was. Walking in that first day on the job, she couldn't help but notice a huge, square table in the center of the room with a giant map placed on top of it. A large woman approached her in an officer's uniform, as she spoke: "Hello luv, put your cap up there, amongst all the others, and follow me." This must have been her instructor, Margaret thought to herself, and so she did what she was told and followed her into the chaos of the room, with people barking orders at one another. As she placed her headset on, a long stick was put in her hand, and she listened intently to what her instructor was saying. After hours of training, it was now her opportunity, as she was walked toward the table, and started listening to the commanders directing the location of the planes. She and the other girls would advance the miniature models around the table with a stick; long before computers and the air traffic controllers of today ~ this was the method that helped win the war. It took a while to master the skills of her job, but with the help of her trainer, and the other girls, Margaret was a fast learner, and caught on very quickly.

Located on the upper deck of the room sat the flight commanders, dashingly handsome in their officer's uniforms, watching the positions of the planes, trying to be professional, as they looked down below at some of the lovely young women working with them. As the girls moved the small scale models about to show their exact locations and flight patterns, more orders came through on their headsets; these tactical movements were vital to the war effort. As she went home that first night from the war room, she realized this would be how her days would be spent, how she would serve her country.

It was dark and cold, when she finished her first day on the job. As she walked across the field from the War Rooms, not too far from her barracks, she made her way inside, and headed in the direction of her bunk; the other girls were all atwitter about some of the men they had met, but Margaret was just too exhausted that day to join in. As she lay her head down on her pillow, she fell into a deep sleep, it wasn't until dawn, the next morning, and the sound of a plane crashing nearby, she was awoken sharply ~ the reality of where she was soon sunk in. As the women ran out of their beds into the freezing chill of that day, they could see in the distance, on one of the landing strips, flames from a plane reaching high into the air, with men scurrying around with buckets of water, trying desperately to douse the flames of the fire and the piercing sound of men screaming, something she would never forget. There were planes that landed back at Strubby Air Base, there were planes that sometimes never came back; so many planes, filled with so many young pilots, some as young as 17, were up in the air, fighting for their country. This would be one of the planes that made it back, but not without a loss for the base of a pilot; and yet life just seemed to go on, planes seemed to fly out and land without a thought ~ the ones that did not return meant a letter home to their loved ones from the base commander.

CHAPTER 3
New Friends

Boogie Woogie Bugle Boy

Often humming away some of the most popular tunes of the day, she had been told many times that she possessed an exquisite voice, so as Margaret grew in her confidence with her daily routines on the base, she decided to try out for the local band that was on the base as a singer. There was already one singer, but why not give it a try? It was a Saturday night, but that didn't mean anything during these war years, civilians generally stayed home, as there was not a lot to celebrate during the bleak war years; but this was Strubby Air Base, in the heart of Lincolnshire, a remote part of the country, not far from the coast. Excitement was in the air, as it was entertainment night, fun songs and singing to be had by all attending. The canteen had been rearranged; tables and benches had been turned to face the end of the room where a makeshift, raised stage had been assembled. All those not on duty for the night had gradually made their way in, until the small room was filled to capacity. No one was going to miss a bit of fun during these times of complete pressure. All went quiet as the base commander made the announcements for the evening, wishing everyone to have a good time. The lights dimmed and a hum of voices went round the room, then it started, a rhythmic beat, gradually getting louder, then a spotlight burst across to the center stage to a lone figure, baton in hand counting down the beat, and with a flourish, both hands came down and the group, as one, came alive as the stage lit up the brass played their first notes.

With his baton constantly waving, the band leader, Bob Potter, brought the small brass section together as they played their first tune "In the Mood," cheers went up from the audience. The song ended and Bob turned, took a bow, and effused, "Hello lads and lasses, we are going to have a fun time tonight!"; with that, he faced the band, one – two – three – four, his baton came down and the shrill sound of a trumpet playing reveille. A spotlight shined on the left of the stage as two young ladies appeared, wearing slightly flared, printed dresses, the hems moving as they shimmied to the microphone and started singing along to "Boogie Woogie Bugle Boy"…..of company B ~ and cheers from the male contingent roared through the canteen. This was Margaret and her friend, Joyce, the singers in the band. When she had approached the microphone for the first time, the wolf whistles from the troops brought a blush to her cheeks, as she looked down and smiled at the sea of young faces, but also a feeling of excitement overcame her, it felt good to be up there, it felt good to be appreciated; she never had been at home! A few couples got up and had a little dance on any open space in the room; tunes fast and slow and some singalongs, and then before she knew it, the time had come to close with the last song, a favorite…."Until we meet again, don't know where, don't know when," tears in the eyes of many who were, come the next day, putting their lives on the line.

For amusement during the war, music brought such happiness into a world that was altogether not very joyful; the band she sang in was small, just six members and two singers. These were such uncertain times and the little joy that could be found would be found in a song. The leader of the band was a man named Bob; he was quite a handsome man with dark brown hair, at about 5'9" he was relatively tall for that time. Bob was held in high regard by all on the base; he was not one of the "fly boys" that the girls would swoon over, but the one man who made sure when the young pilots flew, that their planes were safe. He was a mechanical genius when it came to the planes that left the air base and had to fly over the channel to drop their bombs. When Margaret tried out for the band, it was Bob who seemed to be taken, not just by her voice, but by her stunning looks, and so he decided to give her a chance. They really did not need a second singer, but Bob seemed quite happy to have her join the group, after all, another pretty face would not go amiss with all the soldiers.

After many months of working together, Margaret and Bob had formed a close attachment to one another, he was more of a friend and companion for Margaret, but for Bob, his feelings grew beyond that; he had befriended her the week she arrived and brought her into the group with no questions asked, and now somehow, as the months passed, his feelings had intensified. Her heart, however, lay elsewhere, but that love was not to be.

In her early teen years, she had fallen in love with a man called John Leslie Hardisty-Oldham (known as "Jack" by his closest friends and Margaret), and she was still in love with him; he was a handsome man with wavy, sandy, light brown hair, and he bore a striking pose as a Lieutenant in his officer's uniform. Jack had been born into an upper-class family in Oldham, and in those days, as is today, class distinction is really a part of life in England. Jack's mother, Clara, had forbidden their love. Night after night of fighting between them about Margaret and what was expected from her son; Jack finally relinquished and had tried to honor his mother's wishes and end the relationship with the woman he cared so deeply for, but secret dates between the two young lovers still continued. When either one could get a weekend leave from their bases, they would meet up, stealing whatever happy hours they could get to be together.

Days turned into weeks, and weeks into months; her working at the air base had flown by so quickly and had brought so much joy into her life. All seemed well in her world. By the time she was19, Margaret was still seeing Bob, and yet was in love with Jack. She was a natural beauty, with hair that would drape down her back in soft curls; she would pile the front in pin curls on her head, quite the fashion of the day. With a most beautiful smile, standing 5'4" and the tiniest of waists, she was young and in love. Margaret was working at a job she enjoyed and felt fulfilled doing. It had been just short of a year now since she had been stationed to Strubby and her life had been a happy one since she had arrived. At night there was her band, and great songs to sing, she seemed to have found contentment and happiness for the first time since the loss of her father.

Long days at work and late nights with the band had left Margaret with a feeling of total exhaustion. A constant feeling of fatigue meant a trip off the base to find out what was wrong. Her request for a weekend leave was granted by her commanding officer on the base, and a train trip home over to Manchester would give her the answers she needed. As the engine pulled out of the station, she could see the smoke from the stacks dissipate in the air of the countryside; listening to the wheels of the train turn round and round, while she just stared out the window at the scenery as it went by. This would be her first time back to Manchester in months; Margaret was not thinking of her mother, however, but wondering if Jack would be home on leave, and able to squeeze in a night out; her lips smiled upward, the thought of him just made her tingle inside. It had been several weeks since they had last seen one another and stole some precious intimate time alone, and her coming home would be a complete surprise to him. When finally, after a few hours, her journey came to an end at the station, she picked up her bag and headed in a direction that was so familiar to her; Levenshulme, the place she had been born and spent her entire life. The family doctor on Albert Road would be a safe place to go; surely he would be able to give her the answer.

In March of 1945, two months before the war ended, Margaret sat perched on the examining table, buttoning up the top of her dress, facing Dr. Smith, who had cared for her since she was a child. The news was devastating, as the doctor turned to face her with what conceivably she did not want to believe but somehow, she sensed was coming, she was pregnant. As if in a bad dream, her world came crashing down around her, her life would never be the same from this moment on. Who was the father? She had loved Jack, but turned to Bob when Jack was not there. Times being what they were, never knowing if you would live another day, she had found comfort in the arms of another. The man she loved could not marry her, his family would never allow it, and now she was carrying a child, but whose child?

Bob had proposed marriage immediately when he found out she was pregnant; yet something inside her told her it was wrong; to marry someone without truly loving them was not what she had wanted; it would be so unfair to Bob and the baby. In her heart she had desired a marriage to Jack, so she had turned Bob down. The last time Margaret was ever to see Bob was at London Road Train Station, he was being shipped out, and as they stood together on the platform by the train saying one last tearful goodbye, she couldn't help but wonder if she was making a mistake. The smoke stacks billowing from trains coming and going; all around them people pushing and shoving ~ in a rush to go here and there with suitcases in hand; everywhere you turned there were soldiers with duffel bags over their shoulders, kissing their sweethearts goodbye. As Bob reached out and touched her cheek, her beautiful soft skin, her eyes were full of tears as he looked into her face, the face he had grown to love so desperately. "Please, Margaret, please, for the sake of the baby, I love you". Her head dropped, he knew her answer before it was even spoken ~ there would be no future, no family; as he took a step back, he bent down to pick up his bag; it was over.

The loud shrill of the train whistling twice ~ "Board" shouted the conductor, and as the engines started to roar, Bob turned and climbed up and onto the train, trying not to look back; he did not want her to see his tears. As the locomotive pulled out of the station, he could see in a distance the woman he had fallen in love with and now wondered if he would ever see her again. As Margaret turned to walk away, there directly looking at her was a familiar face, it was Jack; he had waited, out of sight for her to say her goodbyes. She really didn't understand why she needed to see Bob off, but she knew it was the decent thing to do, to end it and not to give him false hope. As she linked arms with Jack and they headed out of the station, she couldn't help but daydream, as young girls do, that he would somehow love her enough to propose.

Being pregnant in 1945 and not married was just not done, or at least it was not acceptable in society. Who could she turn to? Where could she go? Margaret had hidden her pregnancy as long as she could, but the time had come to notify the Air Force of her condition, she could no longer hide her pregnancy. She was immediately discharged; unmarried, pregnant women were not to be tolerated in any branch of the armed forces. As she stood before the base commander, who sat behind his big wooden desk, piled high with official papers, he had seemed so old to her, more like a grandfather figure might be, if she had had one; he now held her future in his very hands. "Private Podmore," he announced in his gruff sounding voice, "There is no place here at Strubby for young women in your condition;" he then picked up his pen and signed her discharge papers in one fell swoop. How strange it was, the women were the ones who paid the ultimate price and not the men when such things happened; men who fathered these children were not discharged. Margaret wasn't even asked who the father was; there would be no repercussions for him. Men were too valuable to the cause of fighting for their country. The men flew the planes, they shot the guns, they sailed the ships, they were just too important to the war effort.

After being released from the Air Force, another train ride back across to Manchester to return to her mother's home was all she could think of. She pondered what her life would bring, how was she going to care for this baby? She already knew the reason she felt ill; but today she felt like being sick, her head was pounding with each and every mile the train roared across the tracks in the direction of Levenshulme. The trip seemed endless, as she gazed out the window at the green countryside; she was desperately trying to think how she could tell her mother the news.

Rebecca, her mother, was a cold-hearted woman, someone Margaret had never been close to all her life. Her father had died in

September 1942, when Margaret was just 17, and the closeness she had with him seemed to only create a bigger gap between Margaret and her mother. As long as Margaret could remember, she had never heard the words "I love you" uttered from her mother's own lips to her; but she had nowhere else to turn; being pregnant, discharged from the Air Force, and with no job, she had to go home. As the wheels of the train drummed on and on, mile upon mile of English landscape just became one little town after another, her heart began to beat faster at the thought of her mother's reaction.

Finally arriving at the train station, the rain was once again bucketing down; "Welcome home" she said to herself ~ "What else is new, rain in Manchester," as she thought about the grey of that day, not just in the weather, but in the greeting that was awaiting her at her Mam's house. She grabbed her suitcase from the rack above her head and stepped out onto the train platform, she pulled up the collar to her coat high around her neck, as to try to keep the rain off her dress; she did not own an umbrella. Exhausted from the journey and the burden she felt in her heart, Margaret boarded the bus and headed for Levenshulme, and her mother's house.

Arriving unannounced, and with no key, she bent down to the plant pot on the ground and lifted it to find the hidden key that had always been there; as she put it in the lock she pushed open the heavy green door to let herself inside, leaving her suitcase by the entryway, she quickly made her way into the living room and lit the fire, so as to warm herself in her mother's home. Both her hands were shaking with not just the cold of the day, but with fear of what she had to share with a woman who had never really loved her. This was the woman she now needed to turn to for help; her heart sank at the prospect of the outcome. As she was warming herself by the coal fire in the parlor, her mother barreled in from the pub and bellowed, "Why are you home?" That was the greeting after months of separation! Somehow Margaret found the words, as she tried to explain the reason for the trip; but the cry for help, from her only daughter, fell on deaf ears with Rebecca Podmore. Not surprisingly for Margaret, came the words from her own mother's lips: The news of her unwed, pregnant daughter, living in her house, was "out of the question, what would the neighbors think?" That was her mother's retort and, unfortunately, the mentality of many people of that time. "Get out, get out now!" she shrieked; "I knew this would happen to you, you are just like your father!" The two women stood screaming at one another, one begging for a safe haven to live with her child, the other with such venomous anger in her heart, that she would hear nothing from her only daughter, not a word! She had to leave the house before she would show; Margaret had to leave the house that very day.

As she climbed the stairs one last time and got a few more personal belongings from her room, she placed them inside her small, frayed suitcase; first a picture of Margaret and her dad that had always been on her dresser since she was a little girl, a special brush and comb set he had given her when she turned 13, and what few pieces of clothing she had left in her wardrobe. War still raging in England, food being scarce and shelter even more so, the dilemma for Margaret was where to go. She left the only home she had known, the home she was born in; as she walked out the door, she turned around to plead with her mother one last time, but no one was there, just an empty hall and a stale smell of beer that always surrounded her Mam and the house.

Margaret ran from her home to the top of the street, the rain pelting down, but now, so much heavier than before, she found the shelter of a red phone box. As she reached in her pocketbook, her hands were cold and shivering as she tried to put the coins into the machine, dialing Jack's phone number; she just prayed that his mum would not be the one to pick up the receiver on the other end. "Dear God," she said out loud, **"make Jack be home."**

CHAPTER 4
Despair

"Never Utter Her Name"

This was a time of total destruction in England, certainly no homes for unwed mothers. Abandoned and on the streets, with no job and little money, she reached out to the man she still loved, Jack. He was the one person Margaret could turn to, the only person left she knew who could possibly help her. He was the one man she knew who had the connections, money, and besides that, the baby was most likely his.

Jack arranged to rent a room for her in Prestwich, a city north of Manchester, with another lady whose husband was away serving his country; he had picked her up outside the phone booth, and as he drove her there that day with the only possessions she owned tucked into the small suitcase she carried, he couldn't help but think what she would do. He had told her he would do the best he could for her, and as soon as she was settled he would visit. Jack had carried her suitcase and held her arm, as they walked up the steps and knocked on the door; she was visibly shaken at the events of the day at her mother's house. A young woman, about Margaret's age, opened the front door; she had a toddler clinging to her frock. Margaret and Jack were shown into a tiny back room downstairs, as she put her suitcase on the floor, she looked around the dismal space, it was a bedroom she would live in for the next few months; she took a deep breath as to hold in her tears. So there it was Margaret lived alone, carrying her child with no family to help her bear the burden whatsoever; her only visitor was Jack, who continued to help, as he had promised, with food and expenses while she lived there. She could not get a job, not in her condition, not without a ring on her finger; what little money she got came from Jack. Each week she would take out a small amount of that money and save it up for when the baby came.

It was in the early hours of the morning when she was awakened out of a deep sleep; bounding out of her bed, trying to pull the wet sheets off the mattress, a pain gripped her like she had never felt before; she knew she had to get dressed and she needed to send someone to the phone box to call for help. She started to cry, she was desperate, no one to comfort her, to hold her up, to do anything for her. She yelled out for help; the young woman who had rented her the room ran down the stairs and out the door to make the call that was needed; the ambulance brigade would be on its way soon. There were no cars to take you to a hospital in 1945, unless you were very wealthy. As Margaret sat on the edge of her bed, isolated in a rented room, with no family for support, she pondered what had happened to her life, and how she and her baby would survive. It had only been a year since her world seemed so perfect, and now it was collapsing in around her; slipping into the only coat she owned, trying desperately to keep away the freezing chill of that fall night, the fire had gone out in her room, and it was bitterly cold, she sat waiting for an ambulance to come. Not knowing what to expect and with no one to lean on, fear gripped her heart, her baby was on its way.

Cold, blustery, winter months were setting in when her baby girl was born in the very late hours of October 17, 1945, at a hospital in the north of Manchester. The nurse had given Margaret something called laughing gas to try and ease the pain, but there was certainly not a lot of compassion for young ladies in her condition. It seemed evident to Margaret that she was being treated differently than the other young mothers in the hospital that night; but it would be over soon and she would have her baby to love. Months before, Margaret had decided on a name, she and she alone would name her baby, it was nobody's decision but hers; if it was a little girl, then her name was to be Janet.

Many days had passed before the charge nurse came to Margaret's bedside with paperwork. The ward was full of crying babies and new mothers tending to their needs. "We have things that need to be addressed," she said briskly, obviously the fact that there was no father had been duly noted by all the nurses. "I need to know the baby's name, please fill out the information on this form." Margaret blushed as she put a line across the box that said father ~ too embarrassed to do anything else; she had made no eye contact with the nurse, she just kept her head down and finished filling in all the lines as best she could.

All new mothers would nurse their infants in the beginning and Margaret was no exception; as she held her little angel close to her breasts, the bonding began immediately, the baby she held was just simply a part of her, a part she now could never let go of. Fear was gripping her with each day that passed by without a visit from her Mam. Over two weeks had come and gone and now the bleak winter days had arrived. She had not seen Jack for weeks, not a single person had come to see them.

The day before she was to be released Margaret's mother finally showed up, and announced she would be back tomorrow to pick them both up from the hospital and then with a swift turn, left as quickly as she had arrived; with not one mention of the baby, where she was or how either one of them was doing.

Early the next morning the charge nurse had brought the baby to her to feed; the time had come for Margaret and the baby to be discharged from the dingy and noisy ward they had spent the last two and one-half weeks in. While she was pregnant, she had saved what little money she had been given from Jack, so she could purchase a knitted outfit to bring the baby home in, and as she dressed her in the white knitted coat and a bonnet to protect her from the cold fall day outside, she pondered on the child she was holding in her arms. She had two little dimples in her cheeks, just a few fine wisps of dark brown hair, and she seemed so little; the things only a mum remembers. She didn't know what she weighed, they never told her, she wondered why, but never thought to ask. She was a beautiful child, everything about her was perfect, her features were so delicate and her skin almost porcelain and as she looked down at her tiny face, Margaret knew she could not face life without her baby in it; but how would they live? How could they possibly survive?

In her youth and ignorance, she thought she was going to be able to bring her baby home to her mother's house, a house big enough to hold both of them. After all, there were two bedrooms upstairs and a front parlor down; and although there was a boarder in the front room, Margaret would keep the baby with her in her bedroom. Surely by now, her mother had forgiven her, and after all, how could you not love your own grandchild? The doctors in their crisp, white uniforms had come that morning into the ward and signed off the mothers and their babies who were going home that day, Margaret being one of them. There seemed such a buzz in the hospital early in the morning, fathers with smiling faces, arriving carrying flowers and suitcases with baby clothes, anxious to take their wives and new little ones home. While Margaret finished getting dressed behind a cloth screen, she looked down at her little bundle lying on her bed, she bent down to pick her up and kissed her forehead; then she ever so gently, unwrapped the blanket from her and began to dress her, for what she hoped was going to be a new life for both of them.

Alone in the small waiting room, sitting in one of the old metal chairs, light green paint on the walls, peeling in places, it was clean, but needed some maintenance; after all it was the war time years and resources were used elsewhere. Margaret had been sitting there for over an hour, but she had not noticed the time as she kept looking down, eyes focused on the small bundle she had in her arms, talking softly, studying and watching every movement of her new baby girl, just loving every moment of it. Couples had come and gone, but now the waiting room where she sat, was empty.

Behind her, through the double doors, was the large room where she had just spent the last two weeks after bringing this wonderful little girl into this world. Typical ward, 20 beds, ten on each side, all open with a walkway down the middle, all the beds were filled with new mums resting, as the nurses got on with their duties. It was 10 a.m., so all was busy, the sound in the air of crying newborns, clicks on the tile floor as nurses scurried around pushing their trolleys full of medical supplies. The first of the visitors were already sitting around the beds, enjoying the special time of the new additions to their families. But alas, not Margaret, she had spent the time loving on her new baby girl alone; no one had come to visit except the doctors or nurses, not even Jack. Why had Jack not visited? Where was he?

Finally, after 90 minutes, the outer door opened up and in she came looking around, "Are you ready? Get your things, we have a bus to catch", chided her mother, Rebecca; no greeting, no how are you? No looking at the lovely baby girl her daughter held in her arms. She turned and walked back out, Margaret picked up the small bag of clothes that was on the floor and clutching her baby, followed her out. Over two and one-half weeks had passed since the baby's birth. Outside for the first time in weeks, it was nice to breathe in some fresh air as she kept pace with her mother. It was a typical November Manchester day, cold and wet. She clutched her baby tightly to her chest, away from the elements, happy inside she was going home.

They reached the bus stop after a ten-minute walk, a little damp and cold, but the baby was warm and dry. This bus stop at least had some shelter, a lot didn't; it was enclosed on three sides and a roof over, protection from the bad weather. A long bench was attached to the back side so at least you didn't have to stand. Margaret sat clutching tightly her baby, her mother sat beside her, still nothing said. A few ladies were already waiting, so a conversation soon struck up all about the newborn, and as it was just after the war, how lucky and difficult it would be for a baby. A few cars and lorries rumbled by, their tires squelching and splashing in the puddles on the rain- soaked road. Soon a double-decker bus approached, number 23 to Stockport Road, "This is the one," barked her mother, as the bus stopped with a squeal of the brakes. The entrance was at the rear, people waited while those on board alighted at their stop, the clippie then shouted,

"Alright luv, you can get on," some went up the stairs to the upper deck, but not this time for Margaret, as that was the smoking section. The smell of stale cigarette smoke filled the air, along with plumes of freshly lit "Woodbine," the "tabs," as they were called, cheap, working men's smokes, constant coughing as people cleared their lungs after each drag, no wonder they were also known as "coffin nails." Her mother led the way in the downstairs section, along the middle aisle until they found two seats together, she let Margaret in against the rain-soaked window, all steamed up with condensation, as she sat on the aisle. They sat huddled together to keep out the cold of the weather outside, Margaret couldn't help but look down on her baby's tiny face and wonder; what would become of her? Everything was dependent on Margaret's mum, who seemed incapable of loving. It didn't take long for the clippie to arrive at their seats, in a smart, but worn, navy blue uniform, a leather bag around her neck and a change machine and ticket dispenser attached to it; "Fares please," came the call, "Two tuppenny ones," came the harsh tone from her mother handing her four pennies, the clippie punched out two tickets and dropped the coins in the bag and with a "Ta, luv," bounded on to the next passengers.

Thinking the bus would take them to her mother's home, and not paying attention to anything but her baby, as the bus bounced and rattled its way down the main road hitting what seemed like every pothole, and there were many. The war had just ended months before her baby was born, there was so much to rebuild in England, including the roads, and it would take years to fix the damage that the bombs had done. The number 23 traveled its route, twisting along the narrow streets, stopping on its way to let people off and on. Finally after 20 minutes, her mother stood up and said "This one," as she worked her way to the back, while pressing the bell for the driver to know to stop at the next point. Margaret followed her, stumbling from side to side as she hung onto her precious cargo, making her way to the exit, she fell backward, then forward, as the bus braked for the stop, the clippie grabbed her to help steady, "It's alright, luv, a got ya." Her mother stepped off the bus, made a quick right and started walking down the street, Margaret was trying to get off and the outstretched hand of a man waiting to get on helped her down.

Looking down the road she saw her mother was now well ahead of her, head down, the rain had turned now into a steady drizzle, so she clutched her bundle tighter to protect it. Her mother suddenly turned left into a doorway, now sheltered and stood looking back as Margaret approached. Finally, she made it to the doorway, stepped in, out of the rain and for some protection, with her spare hand made sure her daughter was dry and okay; then brushed some of the rain from her own face, now taking a few deep breaths to compose herself. Without a word, her mother kept looking at her, so Margaret finally said "Where are we, Mam? What are we doing? We need to get home, the baby is getting cold." With no answer, her mother took a step to the side, there on the building was a sign her body had been covering, in brass letters, "Adoption Agency." Margaret read it, but it did not sink in, her mother threatened, "You have two choices, you take that baby inside and give it up and come home with me, or you keep your baby and you can live on the streets, because you are not bringing that child to my house." Stunned, Margaret could not take it in, she knew she had been cast out of the house before the birth, but she felt sure that the love of a small child would heal all. Margaret started to plead with her Mam, begging to change her mind, promising all kinds of things, just so she could take her baby home. "Mum, I'll be no trouble, I'll look after her, she won't be a bother, just for a while until I can find a little place for us;" but all to no avail, it all fell on deaf ears. Her mother spoke one more time, "The next bus passes here in 20 minutes, either you take that baby inside, or I get on the bus alone." As Margaret stepped inside through the doorway, shivering from the cold, she was overcome with emotion. She tried to reason with her own mind; in her heart, she knew the only way her baby could survive, if her mother wouldn't take her in, would be to give her up to loving parents, who could provide food and shelter; something her own mother obviously would not do, and something that Margaret could not possibly provide by herself. She told herself over and over that it was the only thing that she could do for the good of her baby.

Once the baby was out of sight, Margaret signed the papers; the life she envisioned with her little girl would never be. Her mother grabbed her arm and forcibly dragged Margaret into that cold November day, farther and farther away from her newborn's cry; her breast ached for the touch of her child. As they boarded the bus home, not a word was spoken between the two women, tears pouring down Margaret's face and her mother just staring out the window. What seemed like an eternity, a long journey with empty arms, the bus carried her to the home she had not seen in many a month. There was a familiar smell of beer and smoke, as they walked through the front door of her mother's home, and as she turned to Margaret and roared, "Her name will never be uttered to a soul! Do you understand me? You will never speak of her again." With those words, Margaret ran up the stairs to her room and threw herself on her bed, crying for what seemed like hours until she fell into a deep sleep. When she awoke, her mother barreled into her bedroom and wrapped a linen cloth around her breasts to stop the milk she was producing for her baby; and that is the last memory Margaret has of that time in her life.

The next two years would be a blur to Margaret. Days would turn into weeks and weeks into months. The loss of her baby seemed too much to bear; her heart would just not heal. As time passed and she would walk by a baby or a little girl, she would wonder how her baby was, who had taken her? Every baby's face she would see would be a reminder of the child she had once held in her arms and loved, if but for a brief moment in time. The agony of a broken heart, and a memory that you are forced to bury so deep in the recesses of your mind, this horrific pain was to be inflicted on Margaret by her mother. Would she carry this with her for a lifetime; was this to be her penance for loving so deeply and having this baby? Her heart had been shattered; she had to block that time out in her mind to survive. But never a word spoken, never her name to be uttered out loud again; those were the words that kept ringing in her ears, the words of her mother.

CHAPTER 5
A New Beginning

A Life Shrouded in Secrets

Arthur was a handsome, young Sergeant who had recently returned from serving seven years in the army. At 17, he had joined the Territorial Army; "E Lad, you'll get blown to smithereens!" lamented the two elderly ladies on the double-decker bus, as it headed down the main road, in the direction of his house; but he couldn't help but be excited and proud, he had to tell his mum he had signed up. Arthur was her only son and being a single mum, she had worked so hard to raise her four children alone, and this extra pay packet from the Army would ease her burden, or so he thought. A year later in 1939, WWII had broken out and some six years later, Arthur would finally be sent home from the front lines of battle, back to England. So many of his friends had been lost in the war they had fought; just as those two ladies blurted out, "Blown to smithereens!" They had gone through WWI, and had known what would lay ahead for young men with lofty dreams of fighting for their country.

He had contracted malaria from being bitten by a mosquito, while serving in India, and was still weak from the effects of the disease. Fever, vomiting, seizures and even death occurred in many cases and Arthur was just lucky enough to make it back home, but still in a weakened condition. With so many soldiers returning from the battlefields, there was little, if any, room in the hospitals for them, and so he was to return to his mother's home to heal from the scars of his sickness, and the mental battles of war that so many soldiers had endured. So very many of his friends had not survived! The atrocities of the war were not like you saw in the movies; men did scream and bleed, they did pray and call out for God, for their mothers or their sweethearts before dying. His first campaign had been in Africa under General Montgomery where over 220,000 troops were either dead or wounded. He learned about war at a young age, as did most of the teenage lads, and before he was to leave for India, he was promoted to the rank of Sergeant, something he took much pride in; now, after six long years, he was headed home to Manchester.

In the United Kingdom around six million men were mobilized; called up or volunteered. A total of 700,000 British troops would not be returning home; they had given their lives in the battle to bring freedom to Europe. When Arthur's ship had docked in Liverpool, there were thousands of soldiers who disembarked and went through all the necessary paperwork to be demobilized before they could return to their families. After days of waiting and mountains of documents to fill out, Sergeant Arthur G. Royle was released from his duties, he was now a civilian; he had enlisted in the Territorial Army as a young boy, and had come out of the Royal Artillery as a man of 25. He, along with so many others that day, stood in long lines waiting anxiously to board the buses and trains that would head them home to the safe haven of their families.

Mary Royle was a short, stout woman, standing around 4'11" tall, with light brown, curly hair, but it was her smile that told the true story; her heart was as big as they come. She loved her family deeply, and there was nothing she would not do to provide food and shelter for them; from cleaning houses, to cooking for others, or sewing clothes late into the night, anything to bring in a little extra money that would keep her family together. She had raised four children on her own through one of the toughest times in our history. Her husband Walter had been abusive and had deserted them many years before; Mary had decided, then and there, that she would move heaven on earth to care for her brood of four, three girls and one boy. Arthur had been gone for many years now, and his sisters were busy raising families of their own. Living alone in Levenshulme, Mary had no way of knowing her son had even landed back in England; it had been months since a letter had made it home from the Arthur. There were no phones in the homes of what were deemed "normal folk," and letters took so long to arrive from the front lines. He had sent a telegram to let her know he was safe and headed home by sea, but she had no idea of what day he would arrive, or at what port the ship would dock in; let alone if and when the army would release him after he landed back in England.

Mary almost collapsed when she answered the knock on the door; he didn't have a key, and so when the door opened, she could not believe her eyes; her only son had made it through a war ~ a war that so many sons did not come home from. Almost everyone she knew had lost a son, a husband, a brother or some other family member, and somehow she had been spared that agony. As she threw her arms around his neck, she cried tears of joy; he had been gone six years, but he had made it home. The boy she saw off at the train station was now a man standing before her. He was shivering from the cold of the journey and the effects left over from the malaria he contracted; he had lost so much weight from the ravages of that disease, and he wanted to just sit by the warmth of the fireplace, while his Mam made a hot pot of tea to welcome him home; she quickly busied her hands making some scones, while the pot was brewing, it was one of his favorites; and had she only known he was returning that day, she would have had them ready for him and so much more, she loved to bake for her family. "Good Lord, Arthur, I have to tell your sisters," she beamed; as she raced by him, placing a piping hot cup of tea in his hand and planting a big kiss on his cheek, she made a swift grab toward the hall tree. As she threw on her coat and hat and ran out the door and down the street to tell Lily, Irene and Kathleen~ Arthur had made it home! "Praise God," she exulted, Mary was a religious woman and her prayers had been answered.

It was in the spring of 1947 when Arthur met Margaret; they had both loved to dance, and it was by sheer coincidence that Saturday they would both end up at the local dance hall in town. He had wanted to stay home with his family, but his mother had insisted that he go out with his sisters and other young people and enjoy himself. He had missed so much of his youth with the war, and his mum was not going to let him miss a dance at the local Palais. This handsome young Sergeant was out on the town for a night of celebration after many years of being gone, and music once again, would play a big part in the joy of those post-war years in England; dancing away to the Big Band was everyone's favorite pastime.

Margaret put on her best frock and got dressed inside her bedroom that evening, giving herself one last look over, she was on the way to another Saturday night dance, but wait, her legs, so white, and no money for silk stockings. She ran down the stairs of her mother's home into the kitchen, as usual she found the room empty, her mother was never home now. As she looked inside the cupboard for gravy browning, she found a tin in the back corner; "Perfect," she piped out loud, "This will work!" Adding a little water and making a dark liquid, she began to rub it on her legs. Silk stockings were not to be found during or after the war, and so like most of the girls, they all knew that liquid gravy would serve the purpose and darken them; then a simple line up the back of her leg with her eyebrow pencil would finish the trick. One last look in the mirror and she was ready to go. As Margaret dashed in the direction of the front door, she quickly put on her only coat and hat and whisked her way out and down the cobbled streets to meet up with her girlfriends and they all headed in the direction of Stockport Road and the Levenshulme Palais Dance Hall.

You couldn't help but hear the music in the distance, and up ahead spotting young couples piling inside, out of the damp evening weather. Like all places where young people gathered to dance during the war years, it was a buzz of loud talking, pints of beer for the men, lemonade for the ladies, and always a great live band to play those classic dance tunes. American troops, as well as English, were all around the hall, scoping one another out, hoping to find a partner for a fun night of dancing. As Margaret and her friends entered, the first thing they saw was the sparking crystals of the round silver ball, hanging from the ceiling above, twinkling onto the walls and the wooden floor, as if the lights were dancing themselves. On the stage straight ahead was the band; loud music, laughter and gaiety filled the room as they all checked in their coats on the right side of the hall. The girls would stand on one side together, waiting to be asked for a dance; so many of them in their favorite long dresses and a flower in their hair, but not Margaret, she always opted for a short skirt, much easier to dance in!

That night was to be different; however, as Margaret had spotted a handsome young soldier in his sergeant's uniform and decided to walk across the floor and ask him for a dance, quite a brazen move in the 1940s for a young lady. She declared to him, "My girlfriends tell me you are the best dancer here, how about a spin around the floor?" Little did she know that he had already drunk a few too many pints of beer, and was to trip all over her feet, while attempting their first dance, a foxtrot.

It had been a rainy night when he walked her to the bus stop in hopes that he would make an impression and see her again. As they stood there with other young couples, waiting for her bus, exchanging small talk about the dance and their lives, neither one realizing what tomorrow would bring. Arthur had seen in Margaret, a person he was immediately attracted to; he had missed out on so much being gone all those years, he was shy in so many ways, but he had a lovely sense of humor, and they laughed as they stood there in the cold night air, waiting for her bus to arrive.

He had no way of reaching her by phone, as there were none to be had after the war, so it would take until the next dance before they met up once again. As the saying goes, they fell in love, and the rest is history. He was not to be the love of her life, Jack had been that; but he offered so much more than Jack could ever offer.

Sergeant Arthur Gordon Royle

People fell in love very quickly back during the war years; you realized after all the devastation and lives lost, that time was precious and life was short, so you grabbed hold of it as fast as you could. By April 1947, they knew they wanted to spend their life together and so Arthur proposed on Margaret's 22th birthday, April 14. Passion was strong, war had made it that way; but Arthur was stronger and chose to first get engaged and married. Before a wedding date was set, Margaret had made up her mind, she had to tell Arthur of the baby she had given birth to. He was such an honorable man, his mother had raised him that way; he had fallen in love with Margaret, and his heart broke when she told him the story of the baby who had been taken from her. Between the two of them, they had agreed to start a new life together; they were young, and in love, and they knew there was no way of finding the baby; and so a pact was made between them, something they would keep for a lifetime, they would agree ***the secret was theirs and theirs alone.***

With the war recently ending, everything was still rationed in England, and so a small wedding was to be held on June 21, 1947, at the local registrar's office in Manchester, with just family in attendance and a lunch upstairs at the local pub to celebrate their union. So much had gone wrong in her life, and now a good man, a kind man; but she could not help but think to herself, was she doing the right thing by marrying Arthur? As Margaret put on her suit and pinned a flower to the lapel, she knew she had doubts over her feelings for him, but she could not bring back the past. Jack had left and she knew he was engaged to another. Her baby was gone, God knows where and who was holding her baby now. She would just put sad things out of her mind! That was how she coped and justified what happened in her life.

As she had boarded the bus that morning with her mother, she had known that Arthur was a man who would take care of her like no one else had since her dad, and that thought alone put a smile on Margaret's face. Her suit was grey, cinched at the waist and quite smart looking, or so she thought as she had dressed that morning in her room at home. When they arrived at the registrar's office she was greeted with a chill from the majority of Arthur's aunties; they were angry, he was Catholic and Margaret was not. She seemed far too worldly, as far as they were concerned, but Arthur's mum was delighted, he was in love and that was all that mattered to Mary Royle, her son's happiness. A church wedding should have been first and foremost, in his aunties' minds, but none of them knew the reason why they were at the registrar's office ~ nobody but Arthur and Margaret knew of the baby.

Times were tough in post-war England, there were no homes or apartments to rent, so many had been bombed or caught fire, and so you rented a room if you could find one. Up and down the streets they would walk, hand in hand, looking for a room to let; they had started out their life living with his mum, but they were newlyweds and needed a place of their own. House after house, room after room, all had been rented that day or just before. She was pregnant by now and people were reluctant to rent to a young couple with a crying baby, but finally a room was available. Their landlord was a Miss Harvey, she seemed ancient to them, probably 50 years old, but they were thrilled at anything they could get, so as to be alone. It was an upstairs room and the only bathroom would be shared by all the boarders who lived in the house, the only heating would be a coal fire in their little room. When their baby boy Paul arrived, there was no money for a crib, so the bottom dresser drawer would serve as his cot; so many hardships, but they knew nothing else, it was the norm at this time in the world in Europe and so they were grateful for what they had, for food on the table, and a roof over their heads.

CHAPTER 6
California or Bust

Happy New Year's, Arthur!

By 1950, Margaret and Arthur had two children, a boy and a girl, and there was never any lack of affection or fun in their little family. Arthur loved to take his children to soccer games and stand in the pouring rain with hundreds of other fans, cheering on his beloved Manchester City soccer team. No seats were to be had at soccer stadiums in the 1950s, so you stood for the game, rain or shine, and it was usually rain in Manchester, but just the fun of sharing this time with his children was all that had mattered to him; followed by a brisk walk across the street to the local take out, where they would all share in a paper bag full of fish and chips, sprinkled with vinegar and salt ~ and then a bumpy bus ride home, usually arriving soaking wet, to the chagrin of their mum!

As a young boy in England in the 1920s, Arthur would walk with his pals to the local soccer stadium and try to watch a match through the fence, sometimes the older gentlemen would lift them up and over the wall and place the boys on the grounds to see the game up close; and so it was, he has wanted to share his love of "English Football" with his children and would continue to do so until the very last weeks of his life.

Arthur wanted so much more for his children as they grew, a warmer climate, a better place to make a living for his young family. The world was different in the 1950s, a much safer place; and so in

1956, Arthur sent his wife and now young family over to America, the land of opportunity. He had wanted Australia or Canada, stay true to the flag and pick a commonwealth country, but Margaret would hear nothing of it, California sounded so glamorous, Hollywood was waiting with movie stars like Clark Gable, or so she thought! Arthur packed up his family and sent them on ahead; shortly thereafter he would follow, leaving his beloved England, something he never thought he would do. When you spend years of your life in service for your country, your attachment is so great that it must have been very hard to leave, but leave he must, for he knew his family had to come first. They left behind a lovely, two-story, cozy home, just outside of the bustling city of Manchester, a job he loved, with an office and a secretary, and the freedom to travel around the countryside in his company car; not to mention, a large portion of both their families.

By the fall of 1956, their little family landed in Southern California, and there they would stay. Smog-free air, nearby snowcapped mountains, surrounded a small town by the name of Pasadena. Back in the 50s, the climate was perfect for growing citrus fruits; and a short car ride east, you would find yourself encompassed by orchards as far as the eye could see. The smell of lemon and orange blossoms filled the air with a most fragrant spring scent that only nature can provide. If you drove a stone's throw farther south, you would find a new amusement park being built in Anaheim, by a man named Walt, with the unusual name of Disneyland.

Originally Arthur stayed behind with his Mum, Mary, she had not yet passed the medical to enter the United States; being the honorable son he was; he felt he had to take care of her until she could come to the States, as well.

As he walked his family out on the airport tarmac, that foggy Manchester morning, in the direction of the big, silver TWA plane, it seemed so massive, with its four propellers to carry his precious cargo to New York; he felt a sinking feeling in his stomach, letting go of what was most dear to him. They walked toward stairs at the base of the plane holding hands, and there he kissed them all goodbye. When he bent down, he made a promise that he would be right behind them, and with tears in his eyes, he placed a teddy bear his little girl's arms and gave her one final hug, whispering, **"Daddy will see you soon, Daffodil, I love you, be a good girl."**

This so very kind and gentle man, whose name was Arthur, was my Dad, and I was his Daffodil, whose teddy he placed in my arms.

I can still recall when we landed in the United States of America with Mum; I remember how friendly and kind the flight attendants were on TWA, when we went to depart, giving me handfuls of bubblegum, as I headed down the back stairs of the plane with my teddy bear in my arms. My, how I thought America was going to be a fabulous place to live; I never got handfuls of bubblegum in England! In fact, I had never had bubblegum in my life.

The skyscrapers in New York City seemed so enormous to a child of six years; I had never seen bigger buildings that seemed to reach up into the clouds; and hundreds of people in every direction you looked going one way or another. After retrieving our two suitcases from the terminal, a small shuttle headed us in the direction of the Greyhound Bus Depot. Climbing up the stairs into the bus, the three of us had made it half way through our journey; with big reclining seats, and even a toilet on board, we settled in for our next adventure, as we peered out the windows while it pulled away from the station in New York. Across this vast country we traveled, mile after mile of cornfields, state after state of wide open land, stopping along the way only twice a day meals and bathroom breaks, and to change the driver, for the next trek of the journey. It was such a treat for young children, not so much for mum, while still wearing her high-heel shoes, nylons and a girdle (after all, it was the 50s). With layer upon layer of petticoats under her polka dot dress that had a tightly-cinched waist, mum sat for five days and nights with two very active children, and perched upon her knee was my giant teddy, Edward, that Daddy had given me. The old Route 66 was where Greyhound had placed all its depots with diners attached, and after 3,000 miles on a bus, and no beds, Mum could take no more of either the food or the bus that held us.

It was dark when we arrived at the Pasadena Greyhound Station, and as we stepped down off the bus and retrieved our luggage; we were greeted by my Auntie Irene and family in tow, needless to say, Mum was absolutely shattered. Her feet were so swollen from keeping on her high heels the entire trip, they had to be soaked to try and ease the pain; as she sat on the sofa in my auntie's house, I did not understand why she was crying; this was an adventure to me, a child of six, but possibly the realization of what she had left put fear in her heart, and beside that, those pointed high heels did not help one little bit.

Palm trees that reached up to the sky, something I had never seen in England; the funny part about that was that Daddy had served in the desert commands during World War II in the Africa and India Campaigns; he was so sick of the heat, etc., he was quoted many a time as saying, "I never want to see another palm tree again!" and now here we were surrounded by them. Living in Pasadena made me think we could just walk up to the mountains that looked like you could reach out and touch them; every day was sunny, and so unlike England; you could run outside and play with no coats or sweaters. Mum quickly found a job and we all settled into our new life, sans Daddy.

Seven weeks later, in the wee hours of the morning, New Year's Day 1957, with a beautiful stewardess on either side of him, Daddy descended the stairs of the TWA airplane. With a big smile on his face, and apparently a few too many glasses of free- flowing champagne under his belt, he had finally arrived. Mum, needless to say, did not seem too happy to see him, especially as he had a big grin on his face, as these two glamorous and stylish ladies escorted him off the plane waving goodbye with a ***"Happy New Year's, Arthur!"***

Our first house was purchased in La Puente with $5 down; it was a brand new tract home with three bedrooms and two bathrooms, sheer luxury for us. There was no money for a refrigerator, so milk was bought daily, and put in a bucket of ice in the kitchen. We slept on the floor in sleeping bags until beds could be afforded, but it was such an adventure for my brother and I. The house was surrounded by orange groves and cabbage patches; a haven for a child to play in for hours on end. Capturing caterpillars and any such creature we could find, and not coming in until the street lights came on at night, life just seemed wonderful. Not long after, our Nanna, Daddy's mum, would arrive, followed by Daddy's other sister, our Auntie Lil and her family.

Many wonderful and happy years have come and gone in America, truly the land of opportunity, the rest of our family was to eventually immigrate here with us, or at least **so we thought**! Holidays here were so different in America, whoever heard of a day where you dress up in funny costumes (Halloween) and get given as much candy as you want! Wow, what a great place we now lived in. There was even a Helms Bakery Truck that would deliver freshly-baked, glazed donuts daily to the neighborhood, honking his horn as he went by.....we had truly landed in heaven, at least through the eyes of a child.

The sun seemed to always shine, so when the opportunity of "cheap swim lessons" was given to us by the hospitality hostess lady, as she knocked on the door one day, Mum and Dad jumped on it. With a quick adjustment to learning to speak with an American accent, simply because the kids tease you at school, the years seemed to fly by; summers were the best; they were long and hot and Mum and Dad had done their best to keep us in swim lessons and on a team for fun. We all loved swimming in our family, always have; so one summer day, when Mum and Dad sat the family down on the living room sofa to tell us they had a special surprise, we just knew that it was the pool we had always wanted in our backyard. I asked, "Does it hold water?" "Oh yes, it will hold water!" Daddy proclaimed.....again I ask, "A pool?" ~ Not quite! On March 5, 1961, my baby sister, Elaine, was born, she was my parents' pride and joy, and as Daddy always called her his "Pussycat;" our family was complete, or was it? Oh yes, she was "My pool," she held water!

I was eleven when Mum and Dad brought Elaine home from the

hospital, it was like having a live dolly to dress up and play with. Little did I ever realize that this blonde-haired, mischievous, impatient baby would one day grow up to be one of my besties! We were years apart in age, and before too long I was a teenager, and this adorable little dolly was a thorn in my side when I wanted to bring boys home; she was always around wanting to play. By the way, eventually that pool did arrive, but not in my back yard; I had left home to get married by then, and before I could turn around there was a pool for daddy's "Pussycat" to swim in, Elaine! Go figure!!!

In my 67th year, I am realizing how short our time is on this planet. As I sit down and try to think of all the years and the memories of being raised by two wonderful parents in this magnificent country called the United States of America, it all seems to be a blur; the time went by so quickly. The years of two devoted parents who worked so hard to give their children a better life than they had. Daddy had little, to no formal education as a child, so he had ended up on the factory floor of Ford Motor Company in California, assembling whatever parts needed to be assembled to take home a paycheck for his family. However, in England, he had a wonderful job, with an office and a secretary; you see, he had served his country and had come out of the Army as a Sergeant, so he had a good job waiting for him. As a little girl, he would walk me to school in the morning, singing together silly little songs that made us both laugh; then he would walk to his office.

We were the first family on our street to have a car, Daddy was given a company car, for when he traveled for them, and that was quite posh for those days; remember this was post-war England. No one even had a garage to park a car in, and automobiles were a rare commodity in England for the working class. Our family was blessed enough to have a mum who could stay home and raise us. She was a fabulous cook, it was the one thing that she had learned from her own mother; the only gift her mother ever gave her ~ the love of cooking.

Never was there a shortage of food on the table, and when Daddy arrived home from work there was always a hot dinner waiting for him and two children who landed on him with loving arms. As we grew, mum went to work part time. Many wonderful family memories, and all this time, **“the secret,”** never mentioned to anyone, not even the closest of friends or family, never discussed privately with each other, the hurt was too great for my Mum to even think of it and so **the years passed.**

CHAPTER 7

The Search Begins, March 5, 2013

A Needle in a Haystack ~ One Chance in a Million!

A secret that had been kept for over 68 years had been unraveled before our very eyes and ears; the birth of a baby had been told, the agony and sheer heartache of losing her child. Word by word, sentence by sentence, she shared her loss, what she felt was her shame ~ a life that none of us knew existed. At 93 years of age, our Dad had given us a gift....at 88 years, mum had finally shared her secret.

Elaine's 52nd birthday had certainly turned out to be a surprise for our family; after mum finished telling the story to all of us about the baby who was taken from her arms, she attempted to dry her eyes. With little prompting, she had spilled the whole story in its entirety. Exhausted and tearful, she blubbered, "It's my fault!" Trying to calm her down and not knowing quite how to handle this news, I asked, "Do you want me to find her, Mum?" Looking scared and confused, I really don't think she knew what she wanted, and then she gestured with her head, 'yes'. I decided to start my journey and search for my sister, the sister I just knew had to still exist.

I think back now on what would be if our Dad had not mumbled those few fateful words about **the baby he never held.** I think of all we would have lost, because my Mum would never have told us. Even to this day, she says the shame she bore by not keeping her baby would have been a secret she would have taken to her grave. Mum buried so much in her heart for so long that she was unable to open up that heart, not to any of us. She had been so deeply hurt by her own mother, and so guilty because of her inability to keep her baby ~ she was like a frail sparrow with a shattered wing, except she was a crippled human with a very guarded heart, actually a broken heart, and this was a secret that would be kept until her life ended, if she had it her way.

I now understand so much about my Mum that I never did growing up, you see, if she loved too much, she would have to open her heart, a heart she had closed many years before; a heart that had been broken beyond repair as a young woman with the loss of her child. There was a wall, an imaginary wall, that protected her heart from ever shattering into pieces again. If you don't give your heart to people, if you guard it so closely, if you don't let anyone in, then it can never be broken. It had always been our Daddy who had been the warm one, the parent who picked us up at night and held us when we cried, he was the parent who played the games with you and made you laugh, Mum always was the one who stood back quietly.

With the help of my husband, Keith, we decided to start our quest in England to find my sister; after some extensive searching on the computer, we realized we needed to contact the Director of Children, and Commissioning Services in Manchester, England. The director of this department decided after some time to refer us to another agency also in Manchester, and a gentleman called Phillip. Giving Phillip the information of my sister's birth, October 17, 1945, the name of the hospital, the adoption agency that the baby was handed over to, he then started his search for her. It was like a ***"needle in a haystack,"*** as Phillip was to put it, 68 years later, another country, 6,000 miles away from where we lived, and that was even if she still lived in England. My Mum kept telling us her name was Janet, and so the search for Janet Podmore, born October 17, 1945, in Manchester, England, began; all the time Phillip kept warning us that if she was not in England, there was nothing his agency could do.

Months had gone by, and finally a call from England. "Sit down," said the voice on the other end of the phone, "I have something to tell you." My heart sank as I settled myself into my husband's oversized office chair and took a deep breath. I recognized the voice and the English accent, it was Phillip, and by his tone, I dreaded the words he was about to say. "Are you sure your mother said her name was Janet on the birth certificate?" He said briskly; "Because if you are, there was no Janet Podmore born on that day at that hospital." I could have gone all year not hearing those words; my mother had been so positive that was her baby's name, and that the date and hospital were correct. Trying to gather all my thoughts together, I then thanked him for his help. "Wait a minute, I'm not done," he announced; then, out of nowhere he stated, "I have, nonetheless, found a birth certificate belonging to a baby Podmore." I couldn't believe what I was hearing, then Phillip proceeded to say; "The name on the birth certificate was not; however, Janet, but Daphne, Daphne Podmore."

It took a minute to process this, to realize that he had found information on the birth of my Mum's baby, and that she and I shared the same name. Phillip then continued to explain that this was quite normal for a lot of mums who lose a baby to call their next child by the same name. "What was the next step? How on earth do I find her?" I pleaded. His response was, "Let me send over to you a copy of her birth certificate and we can start the search **now we have her correct name."**

It had been a long day at work and there I was, stuck in L.A. traffic doing my best to get home. Keith had called me with the news, "An envelope has arrived from England," he beamed! I could just imagine the smile on his face. Rushing through the door, he stood in the entry, waiting for me, holding the news. As I opened the large manila envelope, and pulled out the document inside, my eyes read down quickly. Seeing a young woman's signature, my mother's signature, with the name scribbled by it, "baby girl, Daphne," tears just filled my eyes; what would this mean to my Mum? How would she take this? It was Daphne's birth certificate. All of a sudden it didn't matter how long a day it had been now, I rushed outside and got into my car to drive over to Mum's house; wondering if she would feel the same excitement and anticipation I was feeling, but also realizing that now reality of her past was about to be revealed. Mum only lived a few miles away and my car could not get there quickly enough. As I pulled into her parking space at her assisted living facility, and ran in the direction of her building, I was too anxious to wait for the slow elevator to take me to her apartment on the second floor, so I ran up the flight of stairs.

It is funny what the mind does to protect us from a time in our life that broke our hearts, my Mum looked down at the birth certificate and insisted she never called her baby by that name, Daphne; even though there it was, written on the certified copy, Margaret Podmore, and "baby girl, Daphne," with a line through the square for the father's name. "I never called her that, her name was Janet!" she snapped; and then accused me of changing the name on the birth certificate to Daphne. I could see she was upset, maybe even angry at what I had found, but she would hear no more about the name difference and she put the certificate away back inside the envelope. Years earlier, when I was old enough to ask about my own name and its origin, I was told by both Mum and Dad that Daddy had named me; he had known a young lady in India by the name of Daphne and he thought it was just beautiful. Well now, that was a story concocted by them both because of Mum's history ~ she had obviously named me, not Daddy; not too many Daphnes in the world ~ quite a coincidence.

Fall was upon us, and we had been searching for my sister for months, but to no avail. Some seven months since daddy had shared **"the secret,"** and October 17 was rapidly approaching; this particular fall day was to be like no other; we had something special to share in our family that we had never shared before. This October 17 was to be my Mum's first chance to celebrate her child's birthday publicly. The very first commemoration we can have of the baby she had lost 68 years before, the child who was locked away in her heart; she was now able to announce, to tell the world, "Today is my child's birthday," and so with the women in our family, we took Mum out to celebrate. We call her "Daphne 1," as to not confuse her with me when we're talking about her! We know nothing about her, not even if she is still alive, or where she is living, but we decide on this, my Mum needs to have a birthday celebration for her, a celebration she has never been able to have in 68 years. With the women in our family, my daughter Tracie, my sister Elaine, and myself all drove to Mum's house and took her out to a small café in Claremont, nearby her home, for lunch, where we happily acknowledged the birth of her first child, her daughter, a sister and an aunt who lives somewhere in this big world of ours. There is no shame, no judgment, only joy and love. We have not yet found her; Phillip is still searching the records in England, with the hope that she remained living there.

Mum shared with us at lunch that day, that on every October 17 since 1945, she had privately wished her baby girl a happy birthday, and had said a prayer for her. She had no pictures to look at, just a memory in her mind of her precious and tiny face. We all tried to imagine what it would feel like, as we all have children of our own; how on earth do you cope with not being able to share this child in your daily life or with your family? None of us could imagine the burden her heart had to carry all these years. It had to have taken a toll on Mum, and now so many things about her became apparent to me with this realization of what she had kept buried so deep inside; this secret, almost too much for any one person to bear.

By giving her baby up, she gave her life. There was nowhere else to go but on the streets of a war-torn England, and a newborn baby would never have survived in the cold of an English winter; nevertheless, there is guilt in not keeping her, there is fear in the judgment of others for what we all have done.

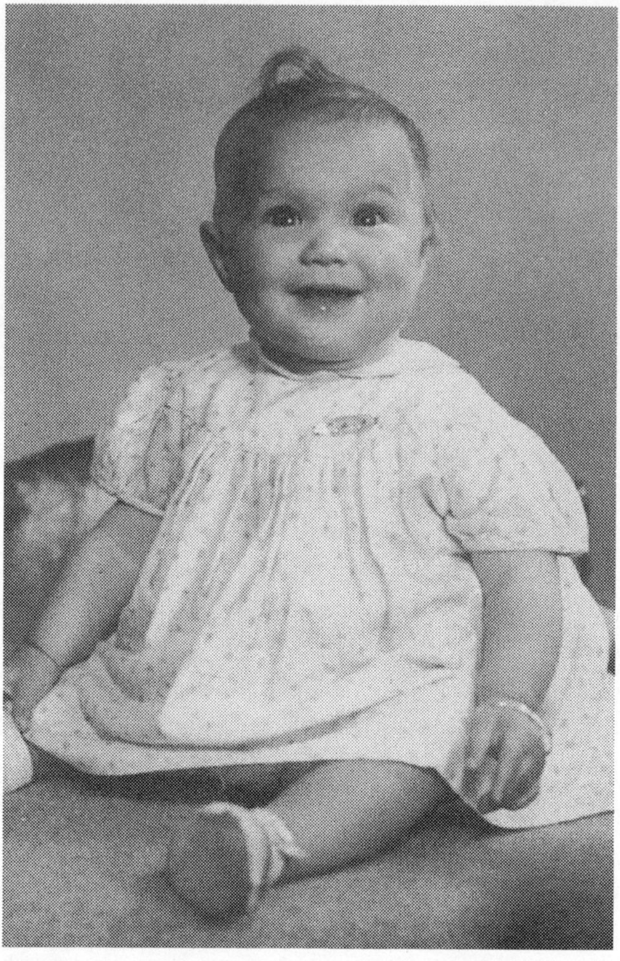

Jan at six months

Months go by and finally another phone call from Phillip announcing, "I have found your sister!" words I had waited to hear. "She lives in the north of England; that she voted in the last election, she is a Nanna, and she is active on Facebook." (This little bit of information about Facebook proved to be a turning point in our search) That is all Phillip can tell me, he can tell me no more; as he utters, "There is no other information in her file that shows she has searched out her birth family!" He prattled on, "Without her searching, the records are permanently sealed, Daphne." However, his agency is willing to attempt to contact my sister with a letter telling her that a "family member" is trying to reach her, and if she is interested, she could call or contact the agency, and they would give her our information. With a definite yes from me, the wheels were in motion, he was to send out a generic letter, naming no names, and we were to wait to hear from him. Weeks go by, still more waiting and no reply, nothing!

November 2013, we have now been searching for eight months and still with no response from the letter that Phillip's agency had sent out months before. The holidays are rapidly approaching and so I once again call Phillip and he suggests I write a personal letter, send it on to his office, he would then forward it to Daphne (as he now calls her). But the information would not be sent until after the Christmas holidays. At this point he insisted, "Nothing that would be so upsetting would be mailed over the holiday month of December by our agency." My letter would lay on his desk until January 2014, when everyone went back to their offices after the holidays.

Knowing that she is active on Facebook and I being unable to wait until the New Year's, and the letter that I had written to be sent, I decide to make my way to the stationery store and purchase two pieces of giant poster board and letters to make a large sign. I make a giant poster that my younger sister Elaine and I can hold up, asking for help to find our missing sister; we stand in the entryway of my home, surrounded by holiday decorations, holding up our sign and Keith, my husband, takes a picture for us to post on Facebook. It is now Christmas 2013, and I am in hopes that she or someone would see the sign and the information on it and contact us. The sign gives out all the pertinent information needed:

"Looking for our sister ~ born October 17, 1945… … … … ….etc. etc."

Daphne & Elaine
Looking for help from Facebook friends

Sometimes what seems like an eternity in life is just a matter of months, but with no positive response either on Facebook or from the agency we were working with, frustration grows. Contacting Phillip once again, he assures me that he mailed off the letter in January that I had written, and he has heard nothing; "Perhaps she does not want contact," is what he is thinking; my heart sinks, because that thought had never occurred to me. So many scenarios had crossed my mind in playing this waiting game, but never that one! Never in a million years, that she would not want contact!

I picture him sitting at his desk, shuffling papers, controlling destinies; he is a "puppet master" over lives of the people he has the power to connect. Day after day, in his office with the life-changing decisions, yet his hands are tied up in bureaucracy. "Why don't you sit down and write a card, don't type it," he proclaimed. "Put something more personal inside, like family pictures." So early the next morning, I sit down at my desk and hand write a card, enclosing pictures of my Mum in 1945 in uniform, the year my sister would have been born. I also enclose photographs, and the story of her birth and of our family, as well as the details of our search for her; I then mail all this off once again to Phillip, for him to forward to her, with the address only he knows.

Months go by, with no response from the Christmas Facebook posting or the personal card I sent. Another email is shot off to Phillip, as he tries to explain what might be happening in her life, he claimed that "She maybe does not want contact; that she is happy in her present life and does not want to look backwards, that she maybe is upset by the past and wants to leave well alone." Now I am getting angry, I can just see him sitting in his office, with a cup of tea in hand, prattling off the darkest scenarios ~ the ones I had never thought of. Something deep inside my heart tells me that this can't be, that he is wrong!

I really don't know why God gives us instinct, but I do know that when He does, we should follow it. Exasperated, I pleaded with Phillip, "Can I possibly get any more help from another agency? Can I hire someone else to help?" Being very British, he took a great deal of offense to this, he felt I was bribing him to go beyond the bounds he was legally able to. I believe it was misconstrued; quite funny really when you think about it, I offended his proper English manners, I must have lived far too long in America, I guess.

You blink your eyes and a year goes by, then all of a sudden it was 2014; a year which found our family struggling with the care of Mum and Dad, now in their late eighties and early nineties. Alzheimer's had stolen the best part of what Daddy was to us all. My Mum had recently been released from the hospital, as caring for my Daddy had taken a toll on her, and her health was failing rapidly; she had been wheelchair bound for some time now with the ravages of Arthritis, and at her age, caring for another had just been too much. The help that both my parents now desperately needed became a precedent over the search for my sister in England. Everything else in life had to be put on the back burner. They both had lived their entire lives, just caring for family and one another, but now family was needed more than ever before to care for them. Elaine and I both were caught up in the day-to-day living and caring for two very special people in our lives, our parents, who had given so much to us both and all our family, it was now time for us to give back. Meals had to be prepared, clothes had to be washed, the house and yard had to be tended and medicines and doctors' appointments had to be kept. Time flew by and, unfortunately, personal time to search for our sister was not a priority anymore.

Decisions had to be made, some very sad decisions; it was necessary to sell our parents' home and move them into an assisted living facility where 24-hour care could be given, especially for Daddy. Elaine and I were still working full time, and so we were unable to give the kind of care that they now required. Weekends needed to be spent holding Open Houses, showing people through their house, in hopes we could sell it for them, along with finding the time to look for a comfortable new home where they could be cared for full time. We managed to find a small complex that we thought my Dad could navigate because of his Alzheimer's. We did not want a large assisted living facility, considering Mum was in a wheelchair, the one we found seemed to fit the bill.

Upon the sale of their home, and the closing of escrow, all that was left was to pack up their cherished belongings, their many possessions, so many memories that they had accumulated throughout their lifetime. The most heart-wrenching thing in life has to be to sort through someone's treasured memories, and make decisions for them that they cannot make themselves. As Mum sat in her wheelchair, and Elaine and I packed up box after box, Mum just cried, it could not all go with them, there was no room, sometimes life is so unfair. Daddy seemed to be more accepting of the moving and commotion in the house; he so often would sit and just bury his head in his books and communicate with us less and less, almost as if he was in a world of his own.

They say "it takes a village" ~ it took our whole family that day to move them into their new apartment ~ but Mum just never settled in; She had lost her " nest," her family home had been taken from her and along with it, any joy she had left in her heart.

As you slowly lose your mind to a disease like Alzheimer's, you forget how to dress yourself, how to put your clothes on or button up your shirt, or even why you need to. We would find Daddy under the bed, he not knowing how he got there or how to get back out; the lack of your appetite other than for sweet food, as if you were a child all over again. He didn't even understand how to bathe himself ~ these terribly sad things and so much were happening in their little apartment. The realization that Daddy's care had to be increased. How do you separate two people after 68 years in the same home? But a memory-impaired unit was what he needed with 24-hour care. His total dignity as a man, as a human being, had been lost and now he was to lose his home with his beloved Margaret.

Finally into a hospice home, where daddy spent his final days, this beautiful home is run by two wonderful women, Becky and Michele, who were the last two angels to care for Daddy on this earth, other than his family. Have you ever found a place where you are meant to be, a place that brings peace to your heart? That is what we found at "House of Grace." We saw a sparkle in my Daddy's eyes that we never saw in the previous home he had lived. Sundays would be spent singing familiar old hymns and this brought a peace to my Dad and our family. There is little more you can ask when you are at this point with people whom you love.

CHAPTER 8

A Hero's Goodbye, September 11, 2015

The Gift of Hope

Life is put on hold, "my rock," my Daddy, our family's patriarch, has died. In the midmorning hours, as Elaine and I lay down beside him on his bed, and sang one of his favorite tunes, "White Cliffs of Dover," his life slipped away. Total devastation hit our family; the unit we had always known would never be the same. So much of all our lives were tied up in this one wonderful man, my Dad.

The tribute to his life, his memorial, was held on Sunday, September 20. The church in Pasadena was filled with people; Daddy would have loved the stained-glass windows of this old, English-style church. Because of the respect for their grandpa, all eight of his great-grandchildren, ages five to twenty, chose to greet the guests at the church door and gave them a program of the service. There was standing room only as you looked up to the altar that was draped in Union Jack flags of England. A true testimonial to his life had been his most precious possession, the framed war medals he was awarded in World War II, that he had cherished so deeply; they now seemed to mean so much more than ever before. The blazer he so proudly wore with his army badge sewn on the pocket, was placed next to his medals, along with all the red, white and blue flower arrangements in the design of the British flag. A wreath of ***Daffodils*** lay next to his chair on the altar ~ the name he had always called me for so many years, now meant so much more to my heart than words could express. Each and every one of his grandchildren told a story, a precious memory; his children did their best to eulogize the dad who was loved so much, but were unable to hold back the tears that just streamed down our faces.

Throughout the service, the wartime music, the music that meant so much to him, played, videos were shown, so many happy memories that his family had shared, and finally, a bagpiper took us from the church playing "Amazing Grace," echoing the haunting sounds that my dad had so long loved. It was the sound of the piper that my father had always remembered during the war; when as a young man in the army, he and his unit were pinned down by the Germans, knowing that there was no hope without reinforcements, sure they would die, and then in the distance, a sound, the sound of a bagpiper leading reinforcements, another brigade was coming over the hill and they would live. The beautiful sound of the bagpipes would always be a favorite of Daddy's until the end of his life.

How do you survive the loss of someone so treasured in your heart? How do any of us go on when we lose those we love? We all have endured this pain, my mother endured it at the tender age of 20 with the loss of her child taken from her; she now endured it again with the loss of a beloved husband of 68 years. God took him home and, in turn, He, unbeknownst to us, was bringing my sister to our family. It's God's timing, not ours. I often think of a poem that I read many years before, and now it is hung on my wall in our house today; it is all about God's timing in our lives. When such tragedy hits us, somehow, in His divine wisdom we are given a gift, a reason to go on, and a reason to live; little did we know, ***our Gift was on its way.***

Our lives to us seem so uncertain at times ~ we can only see the day-to-day struggles that we all endure.....but God sees so much more. He sees the reasons for these struggles. He sees the ultimate outcome of why we must walk through those struggles. In the poem The Weaving, it talks about our ability of only being able to see the dark threads of the loom, the underside, and we question why? Why we struggle? Why tragedies happen? Why we hurt? But you see, God sees the upper side of that weaving ~ the beautiful threads, the finished side ~ the life we will live, and the journey we will walk.

God was seeing the beautiful side of the weaving of our lives ~ the joy which was about to beset our family. The beautiful threads of gold and silver were so visible to Him, but not to us, not yet! We could only see the dark threads, the sorrow we all felt at the loss of such a kind man, such an honorable man, a beloved Dad and husband.

CHAPTER 9

A Milestone Birthday, October 17, 2015

In Ten Short Days, Our Lives Would Be Changed Forever!

As I looked up to the sky, I began to realize how vast our world is, the reality struck me that somewhere 6,000 miles away I have a sister, and today is the miracle of her 70th birthday. There needs to be a celebration in our family ~ something to lift Mum's spirits, to lift all our spirits. It has been 36 days since Daddy went to Heaven, and we all want to somehow give mum a little joy, a reason to go on, a reason for us all to go on. We decide we shall take our Mum out to a British pub in Santa Monica, and there we shall toast to my big sister, my Mum's firstborn, on this her 70th birthday.

Getting dressed that morning, and talking with Keith, I chirped, "What do you think if we try one more time, just once more pulling out that poster board?" We had stored it away in garage and almost given up hope when we all got so busy caring for Mum and Dad. "Why not," he lamented, "Let's give it another go." It had been over two and one-half years since I had first made the board and Elaine and I stood in the house at Christmastime sharing our search with the world via social media. Unknowingly, the first time we tried posting, I had not hit the "public" share button on my Facebook page, just "friends."

It was a beautiful, balmy day, when we stepped outside in the sunshine of our backyard, to once again, hold up the sign; asking for help from anyone who knew of our sister, all the details, the date of birth, the hospital, the adoption agency, etc.; this time it went out on Facebook as PUBLIC! My son Travis is an actor on a show that is very popular in England, and he also posted it on his fan page of some 40,000 more people. As I was walked through the steps of opening a Twitter account with my daughter, I posted for the first time, this tweet, along with my Facebook post is now forwarded to thousands of people worldwide.

Climbing into my daughter Tracie's car, we head down to Santa Monica Beach, instantly my phone started pinging.....and didn't stop! All the way to the beach there was one message after another. People telling me their granny was born on that day, October 17, 1945; their mum was born on that day, their sister was born on that day, etc., all with email addresses or Facebook pages and for me to search, and search I did; one lead after another, all dead ends, with what seemed like hundreds of people to search for over the next few days, still with no positive end result with each and every email that was opened and answered. All Phillip had done was to find her birth certificate and let us know she was still living in England, no more could be done on his or his agency's part, the rest I had to figure out on my own. It was now my turn to do more searching.

I was contacted by the Manchester Evening News and Daily Mirror Newspapers in England, both papers located in the North of England. Their editors have seen the Facebook posting and want to run a front page article in their respective papers for their readers to see and help. What I did not know then was that the particular week of October 17 happened to be **National Adoption Week** in England, and this was front page news. You see, to me this was another miracle, what we in our family refer to as a "God Wink." What are the chances that the week I post about my adopted sister, that it is **National Adoption Week in England?** Both newspapers asked me for Skype interviews and to email pictures over to them so the story could be run immediately. I jumped on it, what an opportunity this was for our search. We knew that my sister lived in the north of England, and that she was born in Manchester, and both of these papers are Manchester papers read by millions of people; but did she still live in Manchester? The article ran in both newspapers that week, but sadly to no avail.

All leads go to a dead end, and as the search for her intensifies even more, at this point we knew we could not give up; we had come so far in such a short time with the help of so many people. As you go through your daily routine of life, working, caring for your own home and those you love, and yet all the time checking your computer for messages and time somehow gets away... .... and then finally an email, someone wanting to "remain anonymous." If I can assure them of anonymity, then they can give me a name! "Look on Facebook for Jan (her last name)," was all they would tell me. My hands can't move quickly enough across the keyboard ~ a strong admonition in my heart was telling me that we had found her, a feeling I had never felt before overcame me. I immediately look her up, it is like looking at my Mum when she was younger; there was an uncanny resemblance to our family ~ this is her, I know it.

I show the picture to my husband, and he immediately dismisses the idea as he chided, "You don't look alike!" Only to learn later on that he was trying for me not to get my hopes up just in case nothing came from it, like all the others, except this time, I know it is her! I send the picture to my son Travis and daughter Tracie...."What do you think?" Immediate response from both, "YOU HAVE FOUND HER"!

I knew she was family, the second I saw this face!

CHAPTER 10

The Final Link, October 27, 2015

A Frantic Search for Hidden Papers

In all my searching, with all the faces you come across, you start to realize how many people live in England and then one day you have found someone who looks like you on Facebook, she lives nearby the city you were born, Manchester, but are you just looking for the similarities to family? She has the same dark hair, the same smile, the same face shape. Are you now so desperate that you think this person looks like you, but really does she? How on earth are you going to now reach out to them? I realize there is no home address on her Facebook page, so I try to friend request her, but there is not a "friend request" on her page either! I decide to go in the "back door" of her Facebook and friend request all her friends to see where that gets me; as I am doing this I tell my daughter, Tracie, who now thinks I am nuts as she utters to me: "Mum, slow down, you are going to scare her off, she is going to think you are a stalker, just give it some time." My impatience gets the better of me as I pace around my living room ~ "I can't do that" is my response! I have never been able to do things slowly once I make up my mind, and my mind had been made up; instinct told me, this was my sister and I was going to find her and find her now!

As Keith and I stare at the face before us on the computer, a face that has become so familiar to us ~ he decides to print out the picture of Jan (formerly Daphne to us). Yes, believe it or not, the name my mum swears she called her at birth, Jan, is my sister's given name from her adoptive parents! What are the chances of that, another "God wink"? Can't tell Mum yet, not until this is all confirmed, but my heart tells me she is the one. So now there is an 8" x 10" glossy picture of Jan, just sitting on my desk at home, waiting to be presented to my mum when we get the confirmation that this is her daughter, her baby whom she had not seen in over 70 years. This is becoming surreal to all of us involved in the search.

Now remember, I could not friend request Jan, but as I said earlier, I did friend request all her friends, one of which, unknowingly to me, was Jan's granddaughter, who would turn out to be my great niece, Melissa. This young lady is the one I call my "Little Link," because without her, this connection would not have happened. Melissa is a young university student who, that weekend, happened to be spending the night with her grandparents. In the early hours of the morning with her phone in hand, as most young people do, she receives a "friend request" from some woman (me), who is looking for her sister, and her sister turned 70 on October 17, 2015, the same day as Melissa's Nanna turned 70! A friend request from America is something she seldom receives, and as she scrolled down my Facebook page, looking at all the family pictures and the one big one of Elaine and myself, holding up the poster, "Searching for our sister," she couldn't help but see the similarities between our family and her Nanna. This was too much of a coincidence, so much so that Melissa tells her grandpa; her grandpa is my sister's husband, Kevin.

Jan had been a baby when she was adopted by the only parents she would know. While playing outside with a cousin one day, she had been told she was adopted and that her name was Daphne, a fact she never knew until then. Running into the house to find her mum to confirm what her cousin had told her ~ was it true? Now faced with the decision of what to say to her young daughter ~ it was to be dismissed, not discussed. Knowing all her growing up years about her adoption, she chose never to follow up on anything. The irony of all this is that the week before her 70th birthday, Jan had mentioned to her husband that she wanted to search for her birth mother, if she were still alive.

It's Monday morning as I am getting dressed and ready to go and pick up mum for a day out shopping, and as I walk into my office to check my computer for messages, I notice an email from Kevin, Jan's husband. October 26 is just nine short days after our second Facebook posting; nine days since I pulled the dusty poster out of the garage and held it up for another chance that sharing it on social media to see if it just might work. The message Kevin had left on my computer that morning was that he needed to verify the surname I had mentioned, as Jan was told another last name other than Podmore; however, all the other information was correct. I stood dead in my tracks, unable to move, staring down at my computer and the words I was reading ~ a man called Kevin ~ a stranger a world away, was checking to see if his wife was my sister.

My next response comes from Kevin, he says that they would "request Jan's birth certificate to find her birth mother's maiden name and hope for a happy outcome" (his exact words) via email. As I sat down at my desk and tried to compose the right things to say, I just wanted to assure him, assure them, that I meant well. I told Kevin that I would send over to him the certified copy of the birth certificate that I have in my possession from the agency I had used in my original search in England and if the one he requested matched, then I have found my sister; I also gave him the information with Phillip's phone number and email to expedite the process.

October 27, 2015, ten days have passed since our last Facebook posting to "find our sister," exactly two years, seven months, 22 days have gone by since Daddy shared those words, **"I never saw that baby, I never held that baby."** How does one simple sentence change your life? In the early hours of the morning, I can't sleep. It is 3 a.m., and something wakes me up, call it a "higher power," some people call it instinct, I call it God. My mind is reeling because I know in my heart I have found her, how can I possibly just lie here in bed when somewhere out there is my sister, and I am so close to finding her, I just sense it!

Looking out at the stars in the sky, my mind thinking back over the journey I had been on for the last two and one-half years, it seems senseless to not get up, and so I decide to go downstairs and into my home office and work for a while. I light the fire to give some warmth to the downstairs rooms, and as I sit at my desk shuffling through paper after paper, nothing can keep my attention on what is paramount in my mind, my sister.

At 4:21 a.m., my phone makes a buzzing sound and as I look down at it, it is 12:21 p.m. in England, and I see an email from Kevin, Jan's husband, I open it up quickly, my heart is just pounding. As I open up the email, I see the words I have been waiting for over two and one-half years:

"You have finally found your long-lost sister,
Your mum has found her daughter."

As I read the words from Kevin, letting me know they are "ecstatic." Jan, according to Kevin, is "a little shell shocked." Emotions just bubble to the surface and I start to cry, and I can't stop. To sit alone, uncontrollably crying from joy is one thing, but it was so much more than that, because the realization of this all coming together was from my Dad and the loss I was still reeling with in my own heart just seemed to come to the surface that morning. How much he gave me, how much he gave our family, was yet to be realized. With his leaving us, he gave us the greatest joy that could have been given to this family, my sister, our Jan. Sitting on my own, in my office, I realize I have found my Mum's child, the baby she was forced to give away over 70 years before, **"A needle in a haystack, a chance in a million,"** as Phillip had said.

I thank God for this miracle, for I cannot imagine my life without Him guiding me through this journey. I thank my Daddy for the innocent words that came out of his mouth that day, some two and one-half years earlier at Elaine's birthday celebration.

The day we found Jan was just weeks after we had lost Daddy; he had gone to heaven on September 11, Patriot Day, a heroes' day that we now all celebrate in America. My father was one of those true heroes, like so many other brave men who served their beloved countries during WWII.

I try desperately to get my wits about me, I cannot call Mum because I am scared I will give her a heart attack, remember it's now 4:30 in the morning, and of course, she is 90 years old at this point. I cannot call Elaine, my younger sister, or my daughter, Tracie, because I am scared they will think Mum has had a heart attack, and I cannot wake my husband because I have been driving our entire family up a wall with this search, but ***she has been found!*** My heart was beating so fast, tears of joy at this news. I am crying and smiling and pacing the floor because I know the joy this news will bring to my mum's heart. The difference it would make in our family was still to be realized.

CHAPTER 11
The Connection

The Past She Had Kept So Well Concealed!

It is Friday, and Elaine always has dinner with Mum each and every Friday, come rain or shine, even after a long and exhausting week at work. She is such a good daughter and as long as the family can remember they have shared this time together. We decide that the family needs to descend on this Friday night dinner with the information we now have, Mum has her first born back. Keith, Elaine, Tracie, her husband, Tim, and myself all show up to dinner that night in mum's dining room where she lives; Elaine presents mum with a beautiful, single-stem, pink rose, with Mum having no idea why. When the dinner is over and the servers are gone, I sit next to Mum and give her the envelope, the envelope containing the 8" x 10" picture of her daughter that has been sitting on my desk; now remember Mum is 90 at this point in time, but still pretty sharp, she opens up the envelope and pulls out the picture and just stares. I can't imagine what was going through her mind, as she carefully pulled out the photograph inside, I beamed, "We found her Mama, we found your daughter," I think she was shocked. She just stared at the picture for the longest time; a myriad of memories of the day she was born, of the baby she once held, of the newborn baby who was taken from her arms over 70 years before, but still the picture of a virtual stranger. I look at Mum and marveled, "Mama, she wants to know you, she wanted to find you," there are tears in my Mum's eyes; her mind had to be reeling with all this information. She said, "How did you find her? I thought you had given up!" I just held her, with not a dry eye at our table.

There were so very many people who had been involved in this process of finding our Jan, not just immediate family, but extended friends from America and England, as well. There are not enough words to thank all who helped from the postings on Facebook and Twitter to looking for addresses, when we finally had a name. I have learned how kind the human heart is, and the joy that we all get from helping one another in this life that God has gifted us with.

In order to start this wonderful reunion, some type of bonding needs to begin for Mum and Jan. Thank goodness for modern technology, we decide to Skype; this is a lovely opportunity, a place to start; a mother looking at a daughter she had not seen for 70 years, a daughter meeting the mother she never knew. Monday, November 2, 2015, they will see one another for the first time since 1945. The computer was set up in our living room, Keith took the day off work to help me with the connections, as I drove over that day to Mum's apartment, I could not even begin to know or understand what she was feeling in her heart and mind. It is a beautiful day, the sun was shining in California, as it usually does most days, and we were all on "pins and needles," my Mum being the most nervous. As I loaded the wheelchair into the back of my car, and got Mum situated for the ride home, she looked over at me and stammered, "What do I say to her?" I reached over to hold her hand, now so frail and shaking with fear and age, I tell her, "Just be yourself, Mama ~ tell Jan about your life, and about her birth; I will be there with you, we will do this together."

When we arrived back at our house, Mum struggled to get into her wheelchair, as I pushed her up the ramp, through the doorway, she turned to me and fretted, "I'm scared." I stopped and wrapped my arms around her for reassurance, I can't even begin to imagine her fears, and I just don't seem to have the right words to say. I don't feel any fear at all, only excitement. But Mum's fears were real, what if her child was angry, what had she done? As Mum sat in her usual place on the sofa in our living room and Keith turned on the computer, like magic, before my Mum's eyes was the child she had never been able to raise, the daughter she had wished "Happy Birthday" to every October 17 for 70 years. There were no tears in her eyes, only a look of amazement of what she was seeing on the screen, a grown woman, a beautiful woman, a mother, a grandmother, where had time gone? It was awkward at first and then, all of a sudden, the conversation just naturally started. One would think that you would not know what to say to one another, and yet they just did, and as quickly as it had started, two hours had passed.

We found out all about the grandchildren my Mum never knew she had, three of them, Lindsey, Paul and Trevor. Lindsey's daughter, Melissa, had been the Facebook link that joined the final pieces of the puzzle together. I mentioned earlier that Phillip, the county worker, had let it slip that Jan was active on Facebook, thank goodness that Melissa was, too. Jan's youngest son's name is Paul; Mum's son is also called Paul. Jan and Lindsey, her daughter, had owned a small boutique, as I have for 28 years. It was as if our lives somehow had paralleled each other. Jan and Kevin had two grandchildren, my Mum's great grandchildren, Melissa and George. Kevin was an engineer, my husband, Keith, was also an engineer before we owned our store. Every time Keith and I would go over to England, we so often stayed with his sister in Thelwall, just a short distance from where Jan and Kevin have lived for so many years. Jan's adoptive mum was named Margaret, also her birth mum's name. Almost as if our paths were meant to cross at some point in time, when all the stars were aligned.

What do you do, and how do you catch up on a lifetime of missing memories? Kevin so kindly sent over to us picture after picture of Jan as a baby, as a little girl growing up and then their wedding pictures, their Golden Anniversary was soon to be celebrated. There were pictures of Jan and Kevin's children and the last was Jan's 70th birthday celebration, and so in turn, we got to show Mum her daughter's life as she grew up, back and forth, videos of special occasions, family events, memory after memory. I start posting on Facebook the news of the reunion, so many people had followed our story, and now a happy ending. It had not been but two weeks before that on October 17, we had taken Mum to Santa Monica and posted a picture with the backdrop of the Santa Monica pier and beautiful blue skies; the heading of "Hoping this time next year there will be another member of our family with us."...It hadn't taken a year, just days, just a few short days!

As the news spread around the world, I got an email from BBC, they are starting a new series in England called "Separated at Birth," and they wanted to know if we would be interested in sharing our story. My answer is, "It is not my story, but my Mum and sister's story;" Jan and Mum would have to make that decision, not me. Being who I am, would I share it "in a minute;" I think this story is **magic** and gives people **hope.** If you think that finding someone who is part of you and part of your family is impossible, then this story proves it is not. BBC goes out to interview Jan in her home, and I get an immediate telephone call from the BBC in England; they think she is a beautiful woman, and this would be a perfect story for their program. They would first film Jan and her family in England; then fly over to America a few days before the filming and interview Mum and our family and would film the reunion at the airport in California. I am so excited for them, for this opportunity, and for other people to see the possibility when you never give up, anything is possible; there are happy endings, miracles do happen.

Alas, it was not to be, Mum and Jan had decided against this story being public. The BBC offer was turned down. I think we all do what is best for ourselves and this turned out to be such a wonderful private family gathering at the airport, coming together with such a small, intimate group with a mother and a daughter seeing one another for the first time in so very many years.

There is a 6,000 mile distance between Manchester, England, and Upland, California. Our Mum can no longer travel far, and certainly not on a plane. Jan and Kevin decide that they must come to America as soon as possible. Kevin will make arrangements for Jan and Mum to finally reunite here in California.

I went to work that Thursday, January 14 ~ my mind reeling with the fact that at 6:14 p.m. I was going to meet the sister I never knew existed. Flight #BA4586 was to land at Ontario Airport; our lives would never be the same from this point forward. Trying to focus at work was impossible, as this was the flight that was to bring two families together and unite them as one. A daughter who was the secret of my mother's past, a sister to Elaine and myself that we had never known, an aunt to so many nieces and nephews. As Jan and Kevin descended the stairs at the airport, their new family awaiting them down below, held signs of welcome. We knew we had to stand back for our Mum, who was seated in her wheelchair, it was almost like slow motion as we stood there and Jan approached her; can you even imagine what was in both their hearts and minds, as they looked at one another for the first time in so very many decades? The Mum whom Jan had never known; the grown woman standing in front of my mother was once the baby who had been taken from her arms so many years before; the baby she had held so close for such a short time, now she embraced and held again as a woman.

Their first touch in 70 years
Mum & Jan

Dreams come and they go in this life, but this dream actually happened, through so many leads with so many people helping, this dream became a reality for my mother and our family. A child taken became a daughter and sister found, and a family bond that will last our lifetime, and hopefully our children's, as well. If you give people the chance, they really do have open hearts and minds when it comes to love.

One simple sentence had unlocked a family secret that had been kept locked away for 68 years....ten little words, **"I never saw that baby, I never held that baby,"** allowed our mum to open her heart to a family that loved her; a family that did not judge her for being human and having that baby, we only felt heartache and sorrow for the loss she had endured for so many years. None of us are without sin. None of us walk this earth without secrets; this secret, my mum's secret, was out, and there was joy in our family and finally for my Mum. No shame, just joy in finding the gift of our Jan.

Mum with her three daughters

CHAPTER 12

Rebecca Battersby Podmore

July 25, 1884 – June 21, 1969

Born in Salford, Manchester, England, she was the fourth child of her parents, Robert Battersby and Ann Rafferty. Two more children were to follow in the family and so Rebecca was lost somewhere in the middle; probably a child, like so many children in the middle, not receiving enough attention, especially with this many siblings in their family.

When you think back to the 1880s ~ there was no electricity, so very little to do after the sun went down. As a young married couple, with no birth control to be found, families were quite large at that time in history, and the Battersby family was no exception.

You wonder where and how our personalities are formed as children, and why some people have loving natures and others, cruel. Rebecca, for whatever reason, seemed to take on the latter. She had come from a lower-class working family, one where the father was gone most days trying to bring home a wage to feed his ever-increasing clan; while his wife had her hands full juggling the six children she had at home, ranging in age from a newborn to an eleven year old. There were two boys, the eldest and the youngest, and four girls in the middle.

Rebecca married young at the age of 19. It was in May of 1904, when she walked down the aisle with 21-year-old Harold Moulden. Not much is known about this relationship, other than they were to have several sons, most of them dying at a young age, many at birth, and two who were to survive to adulthood, Stanley and Harold.

When her first husband died, several years into their marriage, her two boys were in their teens when Rebecca met and married Alfred Percival Podmore in May of 1923, at the age of 38, in Chorlton. Alfred, known as Percy to most of his friends, had just returned from Lagos, Africa, and at the age at 36, had never been married. The newlywed couple had their hands full raising two teenage boys from Rebecca's first marriage; Harold, the eldest, would soon join the Royal Scots Fusiliers, and spend his entire career in the Military; Stanley stayed local in Levenshulme, close to his family.

Their marriage was like oil and vinegar, it just never mixed; they were polar opposites. Percy was kind, gentle and loving, Rebecca was not. When she found out that she was to have another child, as her two eldest were about to leave the house, she was devastated. Percy, however, was thrilled at the news of his first-born child to be. Rebecca had spent her life in the shadows of so many brothers and sisters, never receiving enough attention; so when their baby was born, she was angry at her husband Percy, who chose to give some, if not all, of his attention to their child. Although Margaret was to be Rebecca's only girl, sadly there was never any closeness between mother and daughter their entire lives.

Rebecca Podmore passed away on June 21, 1969, at age 83 at her home in Levenshulme. I now learn so much about this woman, who broke my mother's heart beyond the bounds of my imagination; a woman who threw her own daughter out into the streets, pregnant, with nowhere to go; a grandmother, who turned her back on her first grandchild. My Mum, with the goodness that was still in her heart, cried for her upon hearing of her death; amazing after all her mother did, after all she took from her ~ she still found enough love in her to cry for the mum who broke her heart.

CHAPTER 13
Margaret Podmore Royle

April 14, 1925 – July 25, 2016

Nineteen twenty-five was a world away from the world that we know today, a world of modern conveniences. Back in the 1920s there would be such things as a metal poss tub and mangle, the original version of the washer and dryer, except it was done all by hand, from the scrubbing on a metal board, to the wringing of the clothes on the mangle, all operated manually; then the clothes were hung outside to dry on a clothesline on what would be a hopefully warm day. The oven in the stove was heated by coal, there were no knobs for adjusting your cooking temperatures, your hand went inside and that was how you judged the temperature; what seems like barbaric to us was the norm for the housewife of the 1920s. The bathroom was outside the house, and in England it is cold, and often times a long, wet walk down the yard to an outside toilet. There was no vacuum cleaner for the heavy carpets, instead they would be lifted outside onto a line, then beaten with a broom to get the dust and dirt out of them. Remember, there were no electric plugs in the row house where she and Percy lived, and so candlelight was used after dark to light a room or to read by. Without electricity in the house there would be no TV sets, radios, phones, computers, toasters, coffee makers, hair dryers, curling irons or any of the modern conveniences that we now take so much for granted in the day-to-day lives we all lead; and cars, they were only for the very rich. The chores and responsibilities for a housewife and mother of a working-class family, in that era of time, were very hard; now with a newborn on the way, it would be much more difficult for Rebecca.

She was born on April 14, 1925 ~ Margaret was the pride and joy of her father, but not so much her mother, Rebecca; who at age 40, had found herself pregnant once again. She was two years older than her husband, and now Rebecca would be saddled with his child.

Percy traveled for a living, and so was seldom home, which meant the rearing of Margaret would be left mostly to her mother. A man's job was to provide, and so on the odd times he was not away traveling, Percy would leave the house in the morning and come home late, expecting his dinner on the table, after all, his wife had been home all day ~ what else could one expect?

Wash day was always on Mondays, and very often if there were girls in the house, they would be kept home from school to help out; the mentality of that time was that girls did not require the same education a boy needed. All clothes, after wash day, had to be ironed and with no electric plugs in the house, there was only one way to heat the iron, it was placed on a metal plate on top of the fire in the kitchen ~ a few minutes of ironing and then back on the fire to warm it up again, as it had cooled off. Stiff and starched collars for the man of the house were expected, and Percy was no exception, he needed that for his job. The starch from the potato water was what they would be dipped in, then dried and ironed to make them stand up.

One would think that a daughter born, after having so many sons, would be a delight for a mother, but not to Rebecca, she was just a reminder of the work that now lay ahead for the next few years. When Percy would arrive home from work, he would dote on what would be his only child. He would frequently bring home presents for her from his many working trips away and this would only fuel the fires of anger, resentment and jealously that Rebecca felt towards Margaret. The more Percy did for his daughter, the more gifts he gave his only child, the harder Rebecca would be on Margaret and the more she grew to despise her only daughter. It's truly sad how much withholding your love and affection from a child can dramatically impact and alter the lives of those you love the most; Rebecca chose to withhold her love from Margaret out of sheer jealousy.

Margaret at 6 months

Few memories exist about any of the earlier years in Margaret's life as a very small child. Later on, she remembers, as a little girl, she would play out with her two friends, Audrey and Pat, who lived down the street from her. As children of age nine or ten, they would throw a rope over the lamppost and swing around it, or take a metal hoop from a barrel and roll it down the streets with a stick; simple forms of playing in the 1930s for children. On Saturdays, Margaret and her dad would go to The Grand Movie Theatre for a 6 p.m. showing of whatever was playing; treasured memories of a little girl and the dad she loved so very much. It was her dad who taught her the true meaning of love ~ the endless hours of time he would spend with her, the hugs and the attention that was so lacking from her mother, this made Margaret only love him more.

Alfred Percival Podmore and his precious Margaret
The picture that sat on her dressing table

There were frequent trips to Manchester Train Station, where she and her dad would board the night sleeper down to London, and then on to New Haven, where they would take the ferry across to Dieppe, France. They would then get in a car and go deep into the countryside to meet up with Uncle Frank and Auntie Dolly, her dad's sister. They had two little girls, Margaret's cousins, and they would play for many hours out in the orchards; Jeanniene was her better playmate of the two, the one closer to Margaret's age; they would laugh and share secrets together, as only little girls do. She would climb up in the fruit trees with her cousins and sit and eat peaches for what seemed like hours, while they basked in the sunshine of the French countryside where her Aunt Dolly and Uncle Frank lived.

If the trips to France were not enough, they would be off to Blackpool, a seaside resort town just west of Manchester, where they would go and stay at a local Bed & Breakfast, located just behind the famous Blackpool Tower. Her dad and she were the best of friends ~ he was not just her dad, but he was her life, a link to the love that she had never felt with her mother. Being ten or eleven at the time, it was such an impressionable age for a young girl to bond to her father, and make lifetime connections of her feelings towards men.

She had attended elementary school in Levenshulme, and a scholar she was not! Upon taking her eleven-plus exams; she then went on to finish all her education by the tender age of 14; which was not unusual for working class people at that era in time. There was no hope for a higher education for the working class, especially for girls in the 1930s, you were expected to go to work in a factory or a laundry, and so in her early teens, she was out in the world looking for a job; you were to bring home a paycheck and help with the family's expenses in the house. She would turn over her pay packet, which was cash at that time, and then receive a small allowance back.

By the time Margaret had reached her mid-teens she had fallen in love; the kind that you remember the rest of your life, his name was John Leslie Hardisty Oldham. His parents had owned a movie theatre in Manchester, The Tatler, so many of her dates with Jack would be at that theatre. In March of that same year, her dad had fallen ill and ended up in the hospital. For whatever reason, there never seemed a chance to visit him by either Margaret or her mother. He had his appendix removed, but rather than healing, he got sicker and by the fall of 1942 he was dying; Margaret was never to see him alive again. Not knowing much in those days about peritonitis, once they ruptured there was little, if any, chance for survival.

Much was to poison Margaret's young and impressionable mind as her dad had lay dying in the hospital; a mother who continually reminded the young girl of her father who was a womanizer, who never provided for the home as he should have, but always found time for other women. Her mother had decided, out of anger, or whatever reason, that there would be no tribute for this man. No tears were shed by her mother, Rebecca, for him, he was just gone! There would be no funeral, no memorial, not even a final goodbye. Margaret was brokenhearted; she was wracked with guilt over not taking the time go and see him at the hospital, she never thought he would die. He had been so big and strong and now he was just gone. There would be no closure to his life or the love they shared.

Before she could remember or have a chance to grieve, she was off on a train ride with her mother to a familiar place in Blackpool, as her mother grumbled, "I'll show you what kind of man your father was." A knock on a door at that B & B she had visited so often with her Dad when she was a little girl, then a lady with ginger-colored hair opened the door, a yelling match ensued between the two women and then the door was promptly slammed in their faces. Margaret not realizing what her father had done, the years he had traveled with her and visited other homes of people, coming home as little as possible to spend time with Rebecca, his wife. It went from bad to worse at home with just Margaret and her mother now, no father as a buffer, no more trips away!

She found herself next working at the Manchester Fire Brigade on London Road as a telephone operator at that station, sending out fire engines to where they were needed. The more she could work, the less she would have to stay home with her mother. Jack would stop by and deliver an afternoon meal while she was at work, always keeping the relationship fires burning; knowing that Margaret was suffering bereavement for her dad, he tried to see her as frequently as possible. Jack had lost his father a few years earlier, so he had understood the loss of someone so beloved to your heart. It is strange how relationships can last over the years with one person always pushing away and then dragging someone back into it with the littlest show of kindness. Jack and Margaret's love life seemed to be that way, one where things would be wonderful for months on end, happy times, even during these war years, and then Jack would draw back and then before you knew it, a little kindness, like a night out at the movies or a weekend trip away, and the relationship would start all over again. Margaret very often would blame Jack's mother for his inability to love her the way she had wanted to be loved. The Oldham family name was well respected, old and established in the Manchester area, certainly a girl from "the wrong side of town," Levenshulme, was not what Jack's mother, Clara, had wanted for her son. Margaret's family had nothing to offer, and hence, Jack's mother's dislike of Margaret only grew.

To this day, Mum, now 91 years old, remembers Jack's address: 438 Bury Old Road, Prestwich, Manchester, and even his phone number: Prestwich3024, I often ask myself, who remembers those details? As I sit and write, I am in awe of the secrets that she has kept, and I wonder to this day what is still locked away in her heart. Why this attachment to Jack? What was it that kept him in her mind and memory for over 90 years? Why had she asked me to find Jack now at this time in her life? What did she want to share with him at this moment in time that she never shared with any of us? Was it the story of Jan, although he had known about that baby, or was there more?

They had shared so many memories, they were so young, and so much in love. Across the Irish Sea lay the Isle of Man, it was a favorite destination of Jack and Margaret, and many a holiday would be spent there, enjoying once again the beauty that can only be found in that part of the world. Always sensing Jack's lack of a final commitment to her, and realizing he had a roving eye; yes, Jack had loved the ladies, and when Margaret found letters in his desk drawer at work from not one, but many, reminder of her mum and dad's relationship came into mind. All the ugly things her mother had said about a man who could not stay faithful. Once again she tried to end the romance ~ but life went on, and time went fleeting by, and yet they seemed to always find themselves back in one another's arms; but with Jack's lack of commitment, she found herself in the arms of another man, Bob. Whether it was to make Jack jealous or just out of frustration, she decided she was tired of waiting for him. When she had lost her father, she turned her affection to other men; whether right or wrong, this is what young women do to replace that loss.

When she found herself pregnant, out of sheer desperation, she turned to Jack for help. The baby could have been his, but she was not sure. With no money and the threat of no home to go to, there was no way she could keep and care for her baby herself; she had always loved him and there was nowhere else to go. The war had ended just prior to her giving birth to the baby. The country had to be rebuilt, as all the major towns, including the one she lived in, Manchester, had been brought to the ground with the bombs and consequent fires.

Eventually, Margaret was to find a new love, Arthur, and married him on the first day of summer 1947. Shortly thereafter, Jack married in September of that same year, ironically to a woman named Margaret; the same summer Margaret Podmore became Mrs. Arthur Gordon Royle, Margaret Brown became Mrs. Jack Oldham.

Not too many years later my mum would leave my dad early on in their marriage and go to the Isle of Man, with her firstborn, my brother Paul. I wonder now if that was because of the memories she had made there with another man, with Jack. Had she never got him out of her heart and mind? Who gets on a boat with a little baby and goes to a place where she shared memories with another man? Why? Where did the money come from? Had Jack sent it to her? There was so little money in 1948! My dad sailed over and brought her and the baby back to their home in Manchester, and they tried to rebuild their lives as a young married couple.

My mum's life has taken so many twists and turns; she was to have three more children after the birth of Jan. America turned out to be a wonderful country for the young family to immigrate to. It was hard on mum and dad, but all their children and grandchildren benefited from this wonderful land that we now all call home.

It is amazing that when we keep things buried deep in our hearts, the damage it can do to your own self. When you are a young child, the first people you learn to trust are your parents. Mum's deep devotion to her father and the lack of love shown to her by her mother out of sheer jealousy reared itself when she was but 17 years old, and her father was so ill; the evil and angry mind of her mother was to poison her own daughter's mind against the father she adored. Margaret had not visited him in the hospital because of all the stories her mother had told her. She then had to carry that guilt with her the rest of her life because she never saw him the last six months of his life. An even more evil deed was done by Rebecca to Margaret, the loss of a child, the child she would not allow Margaret to keep.

The man Margaret married, in June of 1947, **Arthur Gordon Royle,** passed away on September 11, 2015, at the age of 95, after 68 years of marriage to his sweetheart, Margaret. They had raised three children in America, all with families of their own. They had taken over 20 trips home together back to the land they loved so much, *their beloved England.*

Janette, Margaret's first born, lives today in Altrincham, England; surrounded by her family, her husband Kevin, and three lovely children, Lindsey, Trevor and Paul, along with two precious grandchildren, Melissa and George. Jan had always told her family the one thing she missed was sisters, she had always wanted two sisters; ironically, she now has them, sisters to share the rest of their lives, enjoying the bond of love they now have found with one another.

Little is known of **Bob Potter**, whether he married and had children or lost his life in the war. Margaret lost track of Bob after that fateful, final meeting at Manchester Train Station, where he once again proposed for the third and final time.

They say every story has a villain, and **John Leslie Hardisty Oldham** turned out to be ours. As I complete this final chapter of my book, I find out more about this man from his family still living in Canada. He was a cold and calculating man, and went through women like water. He had immigrated to Canada with his first wife, Margaret Brown and their young daughter, later only to divorce and marry again in May of 1960; this time fathering four sons by his second wife. Alcohol and abuse ravaged his relationships with those who had loved him the most, his wives and children. He was to marry one last time, and somehow, he managed to outlive his final wife, Mary.

As my Mum had surmised in their love affair, Jack had been a player all along; he had a much darker side than young love could see. He died in Canada, on December 7, 2012, at the ripe old age of 93, with ***not one*** family member by his side.

In the early hours of the morning, on July 25, 2016 at 2:05 a.m., **Margaret Royle** took her last breath here on earth. With her two younger daughters, Daphne and Elaine, and her granddaughter, Tracie, by her side, she went home to be with her beloved Arthur. Loved by all four children she gave birth to, along with so many grandchildren and great-grandchildren, she will be missed dearly.

There are not enough tears that can be shed, there are not enough words that can be spoken or written about this lovely woman; this wife, this mother, this grandmother ~ my Mum. She never got over the loss of her baby girl being taken from her and then finally, the loss of her beloved husband, Arthur.

May you both spend your days in Heaven dancing in one another's arms ~ and maybe look down on the family that you created here on earth with Love, the same Love that we look up and see in Heaven because of you.

Precious nineties ~ Arthur & Margaret Royle

Life takes us in many directions, for many reasons, and most of the time we don't know why, but God does. I now feel like the circle is complete upon writing this story; one of love, tragedy and loss, then the ultimate gain, the gift of my sister Jan, the Last Gift and the most precious of them all.

DEDICATION

This book is dedicated to the two men in my life ~ the one who gave me life and loved me unconditionally, my father, Arthur Gordon Royle; without him I would have never have known about our Jan. Although he never understood what he was telling me on that day in March, it was truly the best gift, and the **"Last Gift"** he had given me, other than his love. The impact that a father has on his children's life is beyond what could ever be written about. I will forever cherish him in my heart and will miss him far beyond any words I could express. The magic sentence he uttered about the baby he never knew, back on that rainy day in March, has forever changed my life and our family's lives. I have never, and will never understand the special bond between my Dad and myself ~ he has and always will be "my rock."

The second man is my husband, my Keith ~ a most wonderful human being ~ who for 30 years has been by my side ~ who has never discouraged me in all I have ever wanted to do, from opening my own store to writing this book. How do you say thank you to those who have given you so much? Little do we all know how much we impact someone with our words; the kindness of them, encouragement with just a hug, the look in their eyes, telling you that they love you and they will be by your side. That is the gift both my dad and my husband have given me.

Love is truly a gift. The love of my life came to me when I was 36 in the form of a gorgeous, English gentleman by the name of Keith Maddison. You have stood by me in good times and in bad, you have raised my children, you have held me when I could not stand on my own, and for that I dedicate this book to you ~ a book of love given to me by my Dad, his "Last Gift."

EPILOGUE

Out of the scrambled mind of an Alzheimer's patient, my dad, a secret kept for some 68 years was unraveled. That secret, and the search that it instigated, brought to many people the realization that so many things in life are possible if you don't give up, that prayers can be answered. Through many twists and turns along the way, a two and one-half year journey turned out to be a beautiful sister, living 6,000 miles away from where the search began. A mother found her daughter and held her for the first time in 70 years; a daughter looked into the eyes of the mother she never knew and found a family who loved her.

ABOUT THE AUTHOR

Daphne Maddison was born in England, and immigrated to the United States as a child with her family. Educated in Pasadena, California, attending the local college, she studied as an art major. She today, has used her knowledge in design to run a successful "woman-owned" business for over 28 years; an accomplished designer, and a prominent figure in the local town of Monrovia, where her boutique, House of Windsor (named for her heritage), is located. She lives today in Upland, California, with her husband of 30 years, Keith, and discovered the love of writing as a way to heal a great loss. She is a first-time author and was inspired to write this book to give others hope in their journey to search for lost loved ones.

Printed in the United States
By Bookmasters